MW01295298

MARKETS & MOMENTUM

MARKETS & MOMENTUM

HOW PROFILING GIVES TRADERS AN ADVANTAGE

JAMES F. DALTON AND
ROBERT BEVAN DALTON

WILEY

Published by John Wiley & Sons, Inc., Hoboken, New Jersey.
Published simultaneously in Canada.

Library of Congress Cataloging-in-Publication Data is Available:

ISBN 9781394318896 (Cloth)
ISBN 9781394318827 (ePDF)
ISBN 9781394318810 (ePub)

Cover Design and Image: Wiley
SKY10093821_121824

CONTENTS

PREFACE

Excellence in any endeavor – whether it's surgery, sports, or futures trading – can only be achieved by balancing the analytical and intuitive powers of your brain. Put another way, you must constantly seek to balance your conscious and your unconscious mind.

There is no finish line, no promised land where you'll always make the right trading decisions. There is only the *process* of seeking opportunities in an ever-changing market structure, and the *process* of making decisions free of the influence of emotional states that have been hard-coded in you, me, and every human being for thousands of years.

Everyone who reads this book will encounter a unique challenge, depending on knowledge, experience, and genetics. Even your current emotional state; how you *feel* influences how your brain creates connections, which then influences how you *act*.

That probably manifests in most readers as a desire to rush ahead to find actionable advice and immediately seek trades. This kind of urge is present in all of us. Unexamined, it has hindered many traders from the profitable careers they envisioned.

Can you put a price on patience? The cost of trading without it is extremely high.

The components of any financial transaction are time, price, and volume.

Only when an understanding of these fundamentals is deeply ingrained can we learn to identify herd behavior and wield our intuition, perhaps our most potent tool.

In order to beat the odds and end up ahead, you must confront the greatest obstacle of all – unlearning preconceived notions that lead to ineffective trading strategies.

> We're so used to doing what we've always done that we don't stop to question whether it's the right thing to do at all. Many of our failures in performance are largely attributable to a lack of self-awareness.
>
> — **James Clear,** *Atomic Habits*

INTRODUCTION

Over the years, I have purchased multiple copies of Shel Silverstein's timeless book, *Where the Sidewalk Ends*. The poem below is one of my favorites.

"Hector the Collector"

Hector the Collector
Collected bits of string,
Collected dolls with broken heads
And rusty bells that would not ring. Bent-up
nails and ice-cream sticks,
Twists of wires, worn-out tires,
Paper bags and broken bricks.
Old chipped vases, half shoelaces,
Gatlin' guns that wouldn't shoot,
Leaky boats that wouldn't float
And stopped-up horns that wouldn't toot. Butter
knives that had no handles,
Copper keys that fit no locks
Rings that were too small for fingers,
Dried-up leaves and patched-up socks.
Worn-out belts that had no buckles,

'Lectric trains that had no tracks,
Airplane models, broken bottles,
Three-legged chairs and cups with cracks.
Hector the Collector
Loved these things with all his soul –
Loved them more then shining diamonds,
Loved them more then glistenin' gold.
Hector called to all the people,
"Come and share my treasure trunk!"
And all the silly sightless people
Came and looked ... and called it junk.

BRIEF BACKGROUND ON THE AUTHOR

In 1972, I held memberships on both the Chicago Board of Trade (CBOT) and the Chicago Board Options Exchange (CBOE). You could say Hector was active in this chapter of my trading career.

Hector was sidelined a few years later when I became Senior Executive Vice President of the CBOE during its formative years. But after I left the exchange in 1979, he became active again.

It wasn't until the late 1980s that I attempted to shut down Hector once and for all when I collaborated with Eric Jones and my son, Rob Dalton, on my first book, *Mind Over Markets;* I stopped collecting every indicator and signal available.

As I read more and more about human behavior, neuroscience, and trading psychology, it became increasingly clear to me that "less is more" – successful trading is about leveraging the *right* information, not the *most* information.

When I became manager of a UBS institutional options trading desk, I began to systematically remove from our quote equipment many of the studies and indicators I had previously accumulated, just like Hector. After some initial pushback, we established a powerful trading desk, and many of my traders went on to enjoy notable careers.

The final confirmation of my anti-Hector philosophy emerged from Josh Waitzkin's book, *The Art of Learning*. Waitzkin was an international chess champion who also achieved fame in the martial arts, and one of his primary tenets was simple: "Depth beats breadth every time." (More on Waitzkin in the "Reading List" in Appendix B.)

In my last incarnation at UBS Financial Services as Director of Hedge Fund Research, I discovered that interacting with multiple hedge funds solidified the "depth beats breadth" observation, changing my trading philosophy forever.

In 2017, I founded Jim Dalton Trading (jimdaltontrading.com), dedicated to advanced trading, mentoring, and education with my partners Jennifer Loh and Raghu Rajput (RJ). Our immersive trading courses and mentoring programs are widely recognized for their breadth and depth. Numerous experienced traders have credited our courses for propelling them to new levels, providing them with a competitive edge by honing their instinct for what motivates their competition, and what drives ever-changing markets. We focus on teaching traders how to cut through the noise – not with magical theories, but by applying a potent combination of observation and practical application to influence probability-based trading decisions, free of biases and bad habits.

My lifelong pursuit of understanding the power of market-generated information (MGI) has been an ongoing labor of love, encompassing many of the chapters shared. That pursuit will continue as long as I'm able to continue to observe the beguiling, often bewildering ebb and flow of price, time, and volume.

HOW THIS BOOK IS DIFFERENT

I wrote *Mind over Markets* more than three decades ago in an attempt to examine and codify my burgeoning understanding of the power of MGI.

When you write, you're engaging in both *external storage* and *encoding*. You're "storing" important information, making it easier to review, while at the same time improving the encoding process that secures ideas in long-term memory. In other words, what you write down has a much greater chance of being recalled again.

> If you can't write about it clearly, you don't understand it.
>
> **—Shane Parrish**

Writing *Mind over Markets* and the follow-up *Markets in Profile* helped solidify and codify my trading philosophy, centered around the visual tool of the Market Profile.

In my early years running a trading desk, when a trade went bad, I handed the trader a yellow pad and asked them to write down their rationale for the trade. If the trader couldn't clearly describe the situation quickly and easily, I knew they didn't understand the trade and I'd give it to someone else on the desk.

At that time, I often spoke about "self-understanding" being a vital component for success, but I must admit that I was painfully light in that area back then. My first two books reveal this dearth, in that there is next to nothing written about how to develop that all-important component of successful trading.

Since those early years, I've done a lot of thinking, reading, and most importantly, *experiencing*. So, while this book has much in common with *Mind Over Markets* and *Markets in Profile*, it represents the culmination of a career spent studying the way humans influence *market* behavior, and just as importantly, how markets (and the constant noise of the modern world) influence *human* behavior.

Importantly, we've eliminated strategies that I've since learned aren't viable. Concepts like "initial balance" and "range extension" – which I once investigated closely – have proven to be misleading and relatively unhelpful. Similarly, I used to detail the various types of market openings, which people loved because they seem programmatic… but they're simply not valid indicators.

I've weeded out those elements.

I was in Vegas speaking at "Traders for a Cause," and a young trader asked how markets have changed. I replied that volume has grown exponentially and hedge funds and large firms now buy order flow, giving them a fractional head start by shaving nanoseconds in order to pocket billions of dollars.

Institutions have always attempted to keep their orders private. Dark pools, which are private exchanges for trading securities, have continued to expand. With the advancement of technology, almost all orders – from single lots to large institutional orders – are entered via algorithms.

Another meaningful change occurred in March 2020 in response to the COVID-19 pandemic, when fiscal and monetary policy led to extreme liquidity. Charles Schwab reported that approximately 15% of its 30 million+ customers arrived in 2020. These inexperienced clients changed the market, contributing to increased volatility. I believe this increased liquidity has been siphoned off by more experienced traders.

But really, the basic components have not changed at all: time, price, and volume are still the fundamental mechanisms of any transaction.

What also hasn't changed – and this is amazing to me – is the continuing dependence on *momentum trading*, which is based solely on price. But a single dimension can never account for the necessary depth of understanding.

The Market Profile opened the door to more readily recognizing MGI. When it was first introduced, I struggled with the relationship between MGI and momentum. I now recognize that they're complementary – momentum is simply the leading indicator, and MGI is the lagging indicator.

MGI PUTS MOMENTUM IN ACTIONABLE CONTEXT

When I wrote *Mind Over Markets*, we were dealing with a novel technology; the Market Profile was a new tool for parsing real-time market activity, and as with any new technology, adjustments, refinements, and a deeper understanding of how best to *employ* that tool have developed over time.

Equally relevant, *Mind Over Markets* and *Markets in Profile* were both written before I had experience teaching traders how to use the Market Profile. I have dedicated the last three decades to mentoring and teaching traders how to understand indicators like momentum through the context of the Profile's constantly evolving distribution curve. This process has been a two-way street, as my extensive client interactions have educated me about the unique challenges that traders face, as well as the best methods for teaching them the fundamentals of market understanding.

In writing *Markets & Momentum*, we've culled both books, eliminating factors that have proven to be irrelevant. We've whittled it down to what is most important, adding depth around *self-understanding*, which can only be developed through consistent effort over time.

It's vital to embrace the fact that the greatest obstacle to your success is **you**. If you aren't aware of the fact that your subconscious is often driving your behavior – manifest in bad habits, illogical shortcuts, and the potent engine of rationalization – then you may be making decisions based on invisible factors.

> Until you make the unconscious conscious, it will direct your life and you will call it fate.
>
> —**Carl Jung**

THE SUCCESS OF THIS BOOK DEPENDS ON BOTH OF US

This book was born of my desire to share the knowledge I've accumulated over a lifetime studying market and human behavior. We'll begin with Part I, a "Foundation" section that establishes key, non-linear concepts that must be internalized before you begin to trade. Read it, take notes (we've included empty pages in the back of the book), and begin your lifelong process of investigating your unique approach to processing information; it is only by discovering how your emotions, subconscious, and layered learning influence real-time decision-making that you can hope to become a successful trader.

Part II, the subsequent "Fundamentals" section will provide you with an essential understanding of the market's continuous, two-way auction process, as well as the theory behind the Market Profile, which is simply an intuitive way to organize and visualize this process.

Many members of the trading community believe I'm a "Market Profile trader." This is not true – I'm a *discretionary* trader who employs the Profile as an efficient tool for organizing the market's unfolding auctions. In all empirical pursuits, the better the data is organized, the greater the odds that you'll be able to glean important insights.

Having worked with traders and clients for half a century, I have recorded many observations. First and foremost: *It's too easy to become a trader*. With a few thousand dollars you can open a brokerage account and, boom: you're a trader. But by most estimates, the average trader's chance of success is painfully small.

> Why do so many people lose? Statistically speaking, it should be impossible for so many people to lose. If the market is random—and most of the time, market momentum is indeed random—why do 90% of clients consistently lose a 50:50 bet? The answer is as simple as it is complex. It isn't the market beating them. They are beating themselves.
>
> —**Tom Hougaard,** *Best Loser Wins*

As you focus on becoming a trader, understand that it's no different than becoming a surgeon, musician, or professional athlete; it's one thing to sit in the stands and critique a baseball game, and quite another to stare down a fastball coming at you at a hundred miles an hour.

> A difficult challenge for short-term traders is that when you become part of a group there is a tendency to become like them. Remember, all the anecdotal evidence suggests that less than 10% of the group is profitable. Our surroundings influence us. We unconsciously become what we are near. As you adopt the behavior of those around you, the changes are often too subtle to notice until it's too late.
>
> —**Shane Parrish,** *Clear Thinking*

PART I

FOUNDATION

CHAPTER ONE

THE SECRETS OF SUCCESS

We often read books as passive observers, letting the narrative wash over us without actively engaging in the experience. This is not that kind of book – you must join me as a *participant* if you wish to gain ground and move forward toward the pinnacle of expert trading.

Even as a willing participant, however, it can be difficult to orient yourself unless you know where you are, as a trader, right now. To respond to this challenge, it's necessary to conduct an honest self-assessment. The following guidelines are designed to assist you in this endeavor.

The majority of successful traders I've known are far more productive when engaging in *go with* trades; they often execute trades in the direction of the salient trend. If they're day traders, "go with" means following the daily trend, or "developing value" (an important pattern we'll address later in the book). Swing traders, on the other hand, tend to execute based on the intermediate, or longer-term trend.

Most short-term, non-professional traders have taken courses that preach "reversion to the mean." They're also taught to wait for signals that confirm a trade. In my experience, successful traders actually *shun* reversion-to-the-mean trades!

In today's fast markets, waiting for confirmation often results in missing profitable trend days (we will discuss trend days in Chapter 14).

SUCCESS REQUIRES CONSTANT PLANNING AND REHEARSAL

In my educational seminars and programs, we frequently refer to "homework," as in, "If you haven't done your homework, you haven't earned the right to trade."

All traders have great intentions, but family, friends, news items, and myriad other commitments and interruptions can transform these intentions into regrets. In order to make progress on the road to becoming a successful trader, you'll have to take a close look at your intentions and tendencies and accept some potentially difficult truths about how you process and act on information. But that's the game. And you either play it with an open, focused mind, or you get played and join the more than 90% of short-term traders who lose money in the markets.

Do you double down on losing trades? This is one of the most dangerous habits inexperienced traders suffer. A wise person once said, "When you're in a hole, stop digging." The use of the word "habit" here, is deliberate. In Chapter 6, we'll review actionable approaches to changing the habits that decrease our odds of success.

Which brings to mind a metaphor that might prove useful as you assess your own inclinations. Neuroscience makes it clear that our standard modes of thought become *physically ingrained*; when we think the same thoughts over and over, we forge neural pathways – superhighways of brain activity that become increasingly easy to traverse.

Changing mental habits is tantamount to scratching out a path through tangled undergrowth away from the highway. The going can be rough.

> Imagine how time-consuming it would be to use a machete to cut your way through thick foliage. A few miles could take days. Once the path is cleared, however, you could move quickly through the clearing. If you were to make a road and ride a bike or other vehicle, the transportation would get faster still.
>
> —**Josh Waitzkin,** *The Art of Learning*

This metaphor is handy because it reminds us that only by *continuing* to beat a new path – through daily practice – are we able to establish new, more productive avenues for thought. As we've established, the superhighway of trader habits does not lead to financial success, so you must ask yourself: *Am I willing to forge a new path through focused, repeated effort?*

Here's a (partial) list of the types of mental tendencies that cause traders to lose focus/time/money:

- Doubling down on iffy trades
- Good old-fashioned FOMO (fear of missing out)
- Unceasing eagerness to take profits
- Fading trend days
- Failure to let profits run
- Reading every bit of news/analysis (almost guarantees cognitive dissonance – addressed in Chapter 6)
- Trusting a "gut feeling" (which is more likely a temporary emotional urge)

The popular writer/psychologist Malcolm Gladwell developed the Diffusion Model as a way to judge where you are most active. The scale also comes in handy when assessing competitor behavior – and your own:

- Innovator
- Early Adopter
- Early Majority
- Late Majority
- Laggard

SELF-ASSESSMENT: WHERE ARE YOU MOST ACTIVE ON THIS SCALE?

Self-awareness is key to being able to combine your skill, experience, and knowledge – the trifecta that gives you slightly better odds of trading with less risk. Few traders process this fact, and fewer still have even thought about it.

But I guarantee: *Self-assessment is the starting point for achieving success.*

In Appendix B, I've listed a number of books that helped me better understand the way I process information, emotions, and the endless noise that courses through our screens. I highly recommend you read them – perhaps even before you continue with this book – to improve your capacity for self-assessment. At least begin reading them in conjunction with this book, as they are an integral part of the experience.

> You cannot change your destination overnight, but you can change your direction overnight. Success is nothing more than a few simple disciplines, practiced every day.
>
> —**Jim Rohn,** Entrepreneur, author, and motivational speaker

CHAPTER TWO

NUANCE

This book is about *nuance.*

My doctor is one of the most esteemed internists in Scottsdale, widely respected for his focus on subtle clues often missed by other specialists. He once asked me what I did, and I told him I wrote books on trading. He responded, "That can't be worth much, because trading – like medicine – is about nuances."

He was wrong to assume that I wasn't nuance-oriented, but he was absolutely right about the importance of those subtle clues that most traders consistently miss.

Nuance means "subtle difference in meaning," and when applied to trading, it indicates the challenge before every trader: *How can I discover opportunities in unfolding market structure?*

Trading is a nuanced art. This book is about learning to find clues in the way the market moves. What follows is a series of observations that create focus areas for your ongoing practice.

FLOOR SCALPERS

"Scalping" originally meant people shouting and gesturing at each other in a pit. This frenetic activity provided liquidity, and scalpers were able to buy on bid and sell on offer with no commission on break-even trades.

Some still endorse scalping as a "low-risk" activity, but the odds are now stacked against you. First, off-floor scalpers buy on *offer* and sell on *bid*, and they're paying commissions – whether visible or not. Scalpers are also up against mega-firms like Schwab selling order flow to large hedge funds. These funds have massive computing power and get to see the public order flow milliseconds ahead of the average trader, their algorithms transforming micro-head-starts into billions in profits.

I have only anecdotal evidence, but it seems less than 5% of floor scalpers ended up making any money screen trading; they no longer had the physical advantages of the trading floor, and weren't able to adopt new practices.

Information on the floor used to come through sound. If prices were going up and the sound level increased, you were likely to see continuation. If price levels were going up and the sound diminished, odds are the rally was coming to an end. Experienced traders almost intuitively had their palms facing the crowd at this point (selling).

Conversely, when trading from an electronic screen, sensory information reaches your brain through your eyes. Many floor traders never realized the significance of this transition.

IRRATIONAL MARKETS AND PREDICTABLE HABITS

Long before I had heard of behavioral economist Dan Ariely, I believed that while financial markets can be irrational, trader behavior can sometimes be predictable. Ariely is known for his work on human irrationality and decision-making, which applies beautifully to the field of finance.

One of the key ideas in behavioral economics which Ariely explored is that people often make predictable, systematic errors due to cognitive biases. These biases can influence how traders and investors behave, leading to patterns and predictability in their actions.

An example of predictable behavior can be found in the way short-term traders get too long or too short – the "Pied Piper syndrome" is alive and well, which can result in trading opportunities when those short-term inventories are out of balance.

Nothing draws a crowd quite like a crowd.

—P. T. Barnum

When I was on the floor, I observed "top-step traders" constantly taking advantage of this phenomenon. This larger trader would recognize that a preponderance of smaller traders were leaning in the same direction. A trader with palms facing the crowd was *offering*, while palms facing inward indicated *bidding*. When a larger trader recognized that the majority was short, he would aggressively bid to force them to cover. As the covering reached a crescendo, the palms would again face outward as he reversed positions.

Pit trading may be a thing of the past, but the patterns of human activity that were once present in the sound of active trading can still be discovered in the multi-dimensional dance of price, time, and value, which we will cover in depth throughout this book.

SCREEN TRADERS

Public, screen-based traders – a small subset of market participants – often follow the leader and wind up too long or too short. Sometimes these out-of-balance positions last for days.

I see this phenomenon occurring electronically as I sit in Prescott, Arizona, watching my screens. Part of successful trading relies on recognizing when these possibilities exist. And if you're unaware, you will likely be caught off guard and end up wallowing in the herd.

We can all be taken in by the Pied Piper.

If I can recognize temporary trade imbalances on my screens, so can hedge funds and large, independent traders. Just as top-step traders used to squeeze floor traders, these market participants now squeeze short-term traders in the same manner. Learning how to read the screen is an art, just like top-step traders learned how to read floor-trader behavior.

There has been a major shift in advantage from the floor trader to the knowledgeable screen-based trader; transparency shifted from the floor to the public. Few recognize the significance of this fact, which is another focus area for this book.

The public has more transparency than ever before. Learning how to capitalize on this is an ongoing process. Like any worthwhile pursuit.

In a very real sense, this is a contest – it's not just about what you do, but what your opponent does. All too often you lose track of this and end up beating yourself. Always make sure you're trading *your* game and not that of your competition.

What you don't do is as important, or maybe even *more* important, than what you do.

ORDER FLOW

Short-term traders often seek answers by analyzing order flow. Years ago, I was a senior officer in a firm that cleared locals, and while I didn't have access to the details, I was informed that one of our locals made more than $5 million executing trades for a premier hedge fund. Large institutional firms go to extremes to disguise order flow.

If they *do* allow you to see their order flow, odds are you don't want to know.

Take a moment to consider, 40 years later, how sophisticated these firms have gotten at disguising their activity in the Internet age of autonomous algorithms.

THE FINANCIAL SECTION

One of the biggest short-term trading traps you can fall into is perusing the financial press; even if you know it's inaccurate or irrelevant, a piece of news that triggers an emotional response can set a bias in your mind that hinders your ability to stay calm, rational, and focused on the information the market is giving you. And you may not even be aware of the fact that you've been manipulated into a biased view!

I had to learn this over and over. And over.

Many traders believe they get value from following economic announcements and the endless analysis before and after a release. But by the time they get the news, larger players have already acted. Individual traders are unlikely to have access to "whisper numbers" – professional estimations from behind the scenes. Even if they had access, the analysis is probably not relevant to their unique trading timeframe.

The press is after readership, and sexy headlines attract readers to sell ad space. Even if you're following a "knowledgeable source," you're not likely to come away with nuanced, actionable information.

For that, you must look to the market itself.

Observe the market's reaction when numbers are announced: These are decisions made by real people with real money. Your best channel for actionable insight is market-generated information (MGI).

Writing this in the final days of 2023, I'm struck by the fact that most Wall Street "experts" predicted a recession this year. These experts were blindsided by the financial strength that actually occurred. Early in the year, JPMorgan CEO Jamie Dimon said a mild or hard recession was possible. Instead, the first three quarters delivered annual growth of 3.2%, falling unemployment, and declining inflation.

My point is this: As a trader, you're on your own.

Yes, I read the financial press, but I do it with my eyes open – I'm a natural skeptic. And, yes, I'm still susceptible to financial biases. Such is the life of a trader.

My experience has led me to believe that the two biggest obstacles (habits) to a trader's success are not letting profits run and fading trends, and these behaviors are often triggered by a headline or passionate pundit waving his hands and declaring something that turns out to be at best a partial point, and at worst completely unsubstantiated nonsense.

In short, buyer (and seller) beware.

MARKETS HANDLE CURRENT BUSINESS FIRST

Any report, news, Fed announcement, etc. is immediately addressed by the market. This action may turn out to be temporary (being aware of this fact becomes more natural over time).

If there's a decent trend at the time of the announcement and the news takes the market in the direction of the auction, there are better odds that it will continue.

On the other hand, if there's a decent trend and the news takes the market in the *opposite* direction, the odds are better that the market will work its way back to where it was before the announcement.

MORE ON EXPERTS

Traders often respond rapidly when an expert gets a microphone. One of my early favorite books was Nassim Taleb's *The Black Swan*. In it, Taleb argues that experts are *domain-dominant*; experts develop in fields that inherently offer a great deal of regularity.

There is too much irregularity in economics and financial markets to enable the development of true experts. There are plenty of *expert claims*, but I find them to be largely overconfident and frequently misleading.

The point is that traders are better served focusing on MGI and trusting their own observations, rather than following "hot takes" from biased talking heads bloviating in popular media.

People are disturbed not by things, but by the view they take of them.
—Epictetus

CHAPTER THREE

CHUNKING

Throughout this book you'll be introduced to terms like "chunking," "neuroplasticity," "ego," and so forth. And since none of us have entered the trading pursuit as an infant, you'll also encounter a focus on *unlearning* – a pivotal component to your success.

YOU MUST KNOW HOW YOU CHUNK TO MASTER TRADING

As babies, our introduction to learning is through sensory information, especially hearing and sight. Through visual and auditory input we begin to develop an understanding of cause and effect; our environment delivers inputs that forge our knowledge of and feel for the world, as well as our unconscious mind, which enables us to recognize patterns and react without being paralyzed by the new and unknown.

These patterns of learned behavior are the *habits* that shape our lives. The importance of understanding the way your subconscious mind influences your behavior cannot be overstated.

> You learn to lock in on cues that predict success and tune out everything else. When a similar situation arises in the future, you know exactly what to look for. There is no longer a need to analyze every angle of a situation. Your brain skips the process of trial and error and creates a mental rule: if this, then that.
>
> — **James Clear,** *Atomic Habits*

Reflect on how excited we get when an infant begins to walk. When that adorably bumbling tyke learns to take those first steps, she is beginning to "chunk" information. *Chunking* is how the brain binds together multiple bits of related information into a single, actionable algorithm.

Can you imagine that baby – or you, for that matter – having to consciously think about every step before taking it? *Let's see: First, I contract my left leg muscle…*

Chunking is how we do everything we do, every day of our lives. For a baby, chunking is running across the floor, squealing with delight. For the expert trader, chunking is recognizing patterns of human behavior in ongoing market flow that enable the placement of trades with slightly less risk.

CHUNKING IS POWERFUL

When I was first introduced to the concept known as "chunking," I assumed it was an obscure psychological term and ignored it. It was almost five years later before I recognized how wrong I was and how important *chunking* is to *learning.*

The simplest explanation of chunking is to visualize a new driver learning to back the car out of a garage. For the novice, this operation requires multiple careful steps: starting the car, adjusting the mirrors, opening the garage door, placing the car into gear, looking behind the car, etc.

After a little experience, however, the brain "chunks" those steps into a single, automatic action. Attempting to work more efficiently, the brain constantly seeks to chunk information, creating neural networks that serve as communication links between chunks.

In his formative book *The Art of Learning*, Josh Waitzkin provided the clearest definition, explaining that chunking relates to the mind's ability to assimilate large amounts of information into a cluster that is bound together by patterns or principles particular to a given discipline.

"So, in a nutshell," he writes, "chunking relates to the mind's ability to take lots of information, find a harmonizing/logical consistent strain, and put it together into one mental file that can be assessed as if it were a single piece of information."

But in its effort to be efficient, the brain can make errors. We'll investigate this more fully later in the book, but training the brain to chunk can be a powerful tool – as long as our chunks aren't composed of partial information we take to be complete, or tainted by emotional biases that lead to costly, hard-to-break patterns.

I CHUNK, YOU CHUNK, WE CHUNK

Chunking can be as simple as getting out of bed in the morning, or as complex as performing your daily market research preparation. These are both routines – either running on autopilot or close to it. When you perform these actions, your brain is employing chunks to reduce the amount of effort it takes to navigate the world.

Conserving effort is something humans *had* to do for eons to survive. If every time you heard a sudden rustling in the bushes you had to spend time and effort trying to determine whether that was a good thing or a bad thing, your genes would not get passed down.

Our brain is constantly organizing neurons and synapses to create these chunks, and they directly affect our daily life experience. And importantly, they influence the decisions we make.

The positive side of chunking is that it allows us to effortlessly move through daily routines. In fact, we would be hard-pressed to even *identify* each of the steps involved in any given chunk! Consciously thinking about each piece of chunked information is inefficient and would slow us down terribly, making us easy lion fodder.

But when the world doesn't respond to the way we've chunked it, there can be serious consequences. For example, when you take a casual step on an unseen patch of ice, it feels as if the world has spun out from beneath you, and your "I'm walking here" chunk fails to enable you to avoid a quick trip to the pavement.

This serves as an excellent metaphor for the danger of chunking the wrong market information, or worse, chunking partial information, arbitrary patterns, or the most common trap of all – what you *hope* will happen as opposed to what is actually happening.

INTUITION AND YOUR BRAIN

I was living in Edgewater, New Jersey, questioning myself after several days of poor trading. I knew the answer was within me, but didn't know how to unlock it.

I drove to Barnes & Noble in search of books on the brain. When I walked in the front door my jaw dropped – there were dozens and dozens of "Books on the Brain" right there on the front display table. My eye was drawn to *Mozart's Brain and the Fighter Pilot: Unleashing Your Brain's Potential*, by Richard Restak, M.D., a neurologist, neuropsychiatrist, and clinical professor of neurology.

Talk about kismet.

My lifelong focus on the brain began on page 41:

> In practical terms, all of the new research on the brain means that no matter how old you may be at this moment, it's never too late to change your brain for the better. That's because the brain is different from every other organ in our body. While the liver and the lungs and the kidneys wear out after certain number of years, the brain gets sharper the more it's used. Indeed, it improves with use. Further, the functional properties of the brain cells continue to be altered throughout adult life, depending on our life experiences.

Until our final breath, our miraculous, mysterious brain continues to change – if we use it. Which means we can hone our *intuition*, perhaps the most meaningful ingredient of successful trading.

The faster information comes at us, the more significant intuition is. Recently as I was returning home one night, approaching the rise of the hill that leads to my house, I suddenly found myself facing a car hurtling toward me in my lane as it passed an 18-wheeler. The car was probably going 90 while I was at 75. What was at work – my subconscious, intuition, experience, or all the above?

News flashes and economic releases can create similar conditions.

For decades I have offered primers, online foundational courses, and intensives for an international audience of traders dedicated to the craft of market understanding. Many of these traders, while well-intentioned, continue to focus on the wrong material.

My goal in this book is to focus on meaningful material whose practical application will assist you in developing your intuition. Our brains are far more powerful than we give them credit for.

It is my premise that intuition grows through the right practical experience.

> Intuition is where it all comes together: it is the indispensable product of our experience, our knowledge, and our will to know and do more. It's my opinion that, contrary to popular belief, we cannot truly experience the spark of intuition in a field in which we have little practical knowledge.
>
> —**Garry Kasparov,** Former World Chess Champion

SELF-AWARENESS (AN ONGOING ENDEAVOR)

If you're reading this section and feeling impatient – *Get me to the examples!* – you are likely headed for trouble. You might pause and assess whether or not you're committed to the work and study and focus it takes to be a professional trader.

> I'm not smart enough to make decisions with no time to think. I make actual decisions very rapidly, but that's because I have spent so much time preparing.
>
> —**Charlie Munger,** Investor and Philanthropist

CHAPTER FOUR

IS OUR TRADING APPROACH DIFFERENT?

The answer to that question is yes and no. There are certainly times to be in sync with the market, as well as times when you should question the market's current direction.

A popular strategy is "momentum trading," which is based on a single dimension: recent prices. Its basic assumption is that assets that have been performing well are more likely to perform well in the future, and those performing poorly are more likely to perform poorly in the future. Momentum trading's popularity is based on its simplicity and ease of implementation.

But a single indicator (price) can never provide the all-important *context* necessary to understand what is really going on. Consider momentum to be a leading indicator, while market-generated information is the lagging indicator. Together they provide a much more dimensional picture of true market intention.

Earlier, we pointed out that entry into trading requires nothing more than a few thousand dollars and an account – there's no required training, certification, or any other barrier to entry. It would be simple to understand the appeal of momentum trading if the majority of momentum traders were inexperienced. However, that's not the case. Momentum trading is strongly supported by many large, established hedge funds; both short- and long-term momentum trading is pervasive throughout the institutional trading world.

The more it's endorsed, the more self-assured traders and institutions become. *Is it possible that momentum trading is the basis for bubbles?*

REGULAR/IRREGULAR MARKET

Over the long term, the market has followed a regular pattern: an upward trend with occasional downturns. As short-term traders, we're faced with quite a different market.

In the short term, markets can be highly irregular, with daily price fluctuations influenced by a wide range of factors, from news to economic announcements and investor sentiment. This sentiment often manifests by being either too pessimistic or too optimistic, and these extremes can lead to short-covering rallies and long-liquidating breaks. Other irregular events – like economic crises, market bubbles, and unexpected news – also contribute to irregularity.

For the uninitiated, this irregularity can be sorely vexing (if not hellish), but for the seasoned trader, it can offer excellent trade opportunities.

PRICE, TIME, AND VOLUME

While there are numerous momentum indicators to guide you – such as Relative Strength Index (RSI), Moving Average Convergence/Divergence (MACD), and Scholastic Oscillator – they are all developed from a single indicator: price.

But price is only a single dimension.

The difference in my core philosophy begins with the introduction of the Market Profile, a distribution curve that incorporates *three* dimensions: price, time, and volume. Price advertises opportunity, time regulates all opportunities, and volume measures the success or failure of the advertised opportunities.

Scientists have always used distribution curves to organize data; the better the data is organized, the easier it is to discover important insights. The Market Profile is simply a way of organizing the market's unfolding auction process in a continuously evolving, three-dimensional graphic. This structure allows the savvy trader to visualize significant market information, like short covering, long liquidation, and overly emotional market development.

Neuroscience confirms that our brains are geared to learn from *visual cues*. The Profile simplifies market-information analysis through graphical visualization, advancing our understanding of what is happening in the present moment, and enhancing our ability to interpret complex data.

THE AUCTION PROCESS

The bids and offers coming from all over the world are distributed via a two-way, continuous auction process. Historically, that process was carried out through open outcry on exchange floors. The world has changed for the better: Bids and offers are now displayed electronically, which greatly increases transparency for the public.

This ease of entry has likely contributed to increased short-term volatility, but most of these new traders have little training and limited experience. They depend on chat rooms, lean on rudimentary technical analysis, and over-emphasize the never-ending cavalcade of news events.

The temporary market convolutions that result from this reactionary approach to trading is where opportunity lies for those who are able to keep an eye on the larger picture, focusing instead on momentum and value as revealed in the market structure.

To illustrate, let's begin with a simple one-way auction from high to low. An auctioneer describes a beautiful piece of art, addressing participants both in the auction hall and on the phone. He initially tries to get the auction underway by soliciting bids for $100,000. No one responds at that price, so the auctioneer attempts to excite the crowd to get bidding rolling, starting lower and finding a bidder at $96,500, immediately followed by bids at $97,000, $97,500, $98,000, and so on until the bids are well over the original $100,000 level.

You experience these auctions every day in futures and equities markets. Reflect on the diffusion model – innovators, early adopters, early majority, late majority, and finally the laggards. *Which are you?*

The auction dynamics continue. If higher bids start to cut off activity, you hear the auctioneer begin to add filler, attempting to make the auction feel exciting despite waning interest. At other times, higher prices attract *more* activity and the auctioneer exclaims, "New bidders!"

A one-directional up auction is still complex, but it only deals with bids. In the futures and equity markets, competing bids and offers are continually arriving from everywhere.

LIQUIDITY AND TRANSPARENCY

The purpose of the continuous, two-way auction process is to facilitate trade among market participants. While screen-based trading provides transparency, multiple strategies employed by larger institutional clients can cloud your view.

Screen-based trading provides a platform for buyers and sellers who assist with price discovery and liquidity – "liquidity" meaning the ease with which market participants can buy or sell without significantly impacting price. The auction process helps ensure that there are multiple participants willing to buy or sell at any given time.

The best, most reliable liquidity normally occurs when the NYSE (New York Stock Exchange) is open (for our purposes, we're referring to U.S. markets). Efficient price discovery and liquidity are greatly reduced during non-NYSE hours. This phenomenon is likely to evolve over time.

Liquidity contributes to price stability. The auction process allows the market to continuously adjust to changes in supply and demand. When demand exceeds supply, prices tend to rise, and when supply exceeds demand, prices tend to fall. While extreme price fluctuations do occur, the dynamic auction process helps dampen major movements.

The auction process also serves as a risk-management mechanism that empowers you to quickly increase or decrease your exposure. While there is 24-hour trading for many instruments, I still observe that liquidity is by far the most optimal during NYSE hours. In fact, the data sample size is simply too low for overnight validation of market activity at this time.

VISUALIZATION

The transition from open outcry to screen trading brought with it enhanced learning through *visualization*. Peter Steidlmayer and the Chicago Board of Trade developed the Market Profile in conjunction with this paradigm shift in trading activity.

Visualization enhances comprehension by simplifying complex ideas. As I have studied visualization methods over the years, it has become clear that visual memories tend to stick in our minds better than text-based information.

Successful trading is creative problem-solving, enhanced through visualization.

In many professions, the creation and interpretation of visual representations are essential. Trading is no exception. Can you imagine architects without blueprints, engineers without schematics, or data scientists unable to use charts and graphs to solve problems?

Visualization is also important for fueling your all-important *intuition*. It helps connect the dots between disparate concepts and divergent information sources, enabling us to make meaningful connections, identify patterns, and reach conclusions more effectively.

Finally, speed and reaction times are vital – especially for short-term trading. Being able to visualize developing market conditions can provide an advantage, and that is where the bulk of the "Fundamentals" section will focus.

> The formulation of the problem is often more essential than its solution.
> —**Albert Einstein**

CHAPTER FIVE

MARKET UNDERSTANDING ONLY GOES SO FAR

Emotional intelligence, also known as emotional quotient (EQ), is your ability to understand and manage your emotions. EQ is instrumental in communicating effectively and overcoming challenges. The only way to achieve trading success is by combining *market* understanding with *self*-understanding, and EQ is an integral component of the latter.

As I admitted in the Introduction, self-understanding was perhaps the most prominent barrier to my early trading efforts. Despite a well-developed rigor for observing and evaluating market-generated information, I often let my emotions skew my decisions toward factors like *availability bias* (relying too much on what readily comes to mind) and *recency bias* (over-emphasizing the latest information when estimating future events). These undiagnosed biases were detrimental to my profitability.

In the early chapters of my career, I was a *counter-trend* trader. In retrospect, my ego was leading the way, as I generally believed I was smarter than the market. This narrow-minded approach kept me from developing a broader perspective, and the results made it clear I needed to seek a new approach to trading.

Day trading is a volatile, high-pressure endeavor. It involves making rapid decisions based on subtle market indicators. Having a well-developed EQ enhances your ability to navigate this process effectively.

KNOW THYSELF

Self-awareness, a key component of EQ, is necessary to first *recognize* and then *manage* your shifting emotional states. You might be influenced by apprehension when the market moves against a trade. You could feel a surge of greed when you start doing make-believe math when things swing your way.

These emotions lead to impulsive decisions. Acknowledgment is the starting point.

Traders with high self-awareness can better understand and control their emotional responses, preventing rash actions from doing serious financial damage.

Emotional *resilience* is another key component of successful trading. We all make bad decisions. We all get unduly influenced by *confirmation bias*, when we look for proof of our preconceived notions, ignoring anything that tells a different story.

The ability to bounce back from these setbacks, losses, and unexpected market shifts is vital for getting clear-headed for the next trade. And the one after that.

You can advance your self-understanding by *expressing* the shifting nature of your emotional states; when you write down your feelings, it becomes easier to understand and reckon with them. Over time, you'll get better at recognizing those times when you're riled, when you're not trading from a calm, balanced perspective.

And in those times, you'll make an important decision: *You won't trade.*

A positive practice you can adopt to make progress on the road to expert trading is to keep a detailed trade journal, carefully noting the circumstances, assumptions, and emotional states you were experiencing before, during, and after every trade. Over time, you will begin to see patterns and learn how to focus your attention to improve your odds of success. We'll discuss journaling in more detail at the end of the book.

> It may not be possible to know who you are without somehow expressing it.
>
> —**Rick Rubin,** Author and Legendary Record Producer

The story you tell yourself is the most powerful influence in the world. The stories we tell ourselves about the events that unfold in our lives become our "truths," and if we're not careful, we can build decision-making systems on a shaky foundation of unfounded opinions and emotional surges that can codify erroneous beliefs.

Eventually we start believing, even if the stories we tell ourselves are not true.

BE HERE NOW

No matter how you have come to a decision, you ultimately make that decision in the present moment – the only "time" in which you have any power to influence your fate. We can spend endless hours worrying over the past or trying to guess at the future, but it is only in the "now" that we are actually alive and able to express our agency.

When a trade goes badly, it's easy to get knocked back on your heels, consumed with worry that it will happen again. That's why so many traders make cardinal errors, holding onto losing trades in hopes that they'll turn around (hope) or taking profits too soon, before a trade has a chance to develop (fear).

One of the most powerful steps you can take to becoming a successful trader is to embrace a process – and it's different for every individual – that enables you to let go of past trades, both good and bad, in order to focus on what is actually happening, right now, in the market unfolding before you.

Not what you hope is happening. Not what you fear might occur.

That's where the power of market-generated information is key, because it can serve as a doorway to the present moment.

My first educational effort was a tape set entitled "Operating in the Present Tense." Once it was released, I received accusations that I was parroting Phil Jackson, head coach of the Chicago Bulls during their 1990's NBA championship runs. I lived in Chicago and was certainly a Bulls fan, but had not read Phil's book at that point.

I have read his book since, and entirely agree with his philosophy.

> The secret of the Bull's success was dealing in the present tense. Play the current game, not yesterday's or tomorrow's.
>
> **—Phil Jackson**

YOUR BRAIN IS PLASTIC

"Neural plasticity" is the fundamental property of the brain that enables endless reconfiguring of synaptic connections based on environmental inputs, mediated by your focus. Your brain has an inherent potential for transformation; *where* you pay attention becomes *who* you are.

Understanding the *malleability* of neural circuits illuminates the remarkable capacity of the brain to adapt and reshape itself in response to experiences. Comprehending this plasticity reframes our understanding of learning and adaptation.

The brain refines neural connections based on the consequences of every decision you make. Poor decisions, when repeated, become a neural superhighway that makes it even easier to rationalize and make up stories about what you'd *like* to happen, rather than what is actually happening.

The recognition that neural circuits can be rewired encourages a more considered approach to decision-making; a continuous exploration of our own subjective experience fosters *cognitive agility* and resilience in the face of dynamic challenges.

Neuroscience reveals that deliberate engagement – when we're focused on objective, actionable information – refines neural pathways, enhancing cognitive functions that influence the way we make decisions.

Understanding the brain's plastic nature enables us to mold our cognitive landscape. We can improve the clarity of our focus. We can make less emotional decisions.

> There is an enormous difference between being hostage to one's thoughts and being freely and nonjudgmentally aware of life in the present.
>
> —**Sam Harris,** Philosopher, Neuroscientist, and Author

Forge a new neural network before your next trade: Create a new routine that involves thorough preparation prior to the market opening. Keep notes as you develop this new practice, so you can track your progress and hold yourself accountable.

Personal momentum is more important than market momentum. Many traders give up on preparation and homework when the results aren't immediate. Just a couple percent points of change become significant after you've been doing it for six months.

CHAPTER SIX

YOU CAN'T ALWAYS FORGET WHAT YOU WANT

Even with a plastic brain, it's challenging to unlearn behaviors, especially when they've been repeated year after year.

It's estimated that less than 10% of short-term traders make money. And it's unlikely that it's the same 10% from one year to the next. When I ran a discount futures brokerage firm in the 1980s, the average account lasted just seven weeks!

Consider again the metaphor of the superhighway that represents "the way you've always done it," the dominant patterns of your mind. Now you're tasked with scratching out a new route through untamed wilderness. The good news is that we can pave these new pathways toward more objective, rational ends.

But it takes courage to change.

In order to unlearn counterproductive habits, you must invest the time required to observe and understand your own behaviors. In that pursuit, it can be helpful to understand the mechanisms of unlearning.

The most powerful tool for changing cognitive behaviors is known as "pruning." As we dedicate effort to learning new things, your brain strengthens connections between neurons in active use, while weakening connections between those no longer required to fire – all depending on where we train our *active focus*. This "pruning" process effectively pares away thought processes that are no longer useful.

Reading this book will help rewire your brain. In the ensuing Part II, "Fundamentals," I'll be sharing specific examples of patterns that allow you to take advantage of temporary imbalances in unfolding market structure. By studying these new concepts and practices, you'll be triggering your "mirror neuron" system, which activates when we observe someone performing an action. We can learn new skills and behaviors through imitation.

UNLEARNING IS HARD

Brain science is fascinating, and it helps rub away at the fogged mirror so we can better understand the way we respond to the world. A better self-understanding also helps motivate us through the slow, effortful process of changing behaviors – we can use our powerful rationalization engine to remind ourselves that this focused attention, over time, will break bad habits and overcome the biases that prevent us from seeing clearly what is happening in real time.

The biggest obstacle to unlearning is *mental inertia*; our brains tend to stick to established patterns and knowledge. That tendency saved our lives when the challenge was daily survival, but in a modern digital context, it can be catastrophic.

We also become emotionally attached to beliefs. We involve our ego, associating our own worth with opinions we may not even be able to support. Letting go of these ideas can be uncomfortable – they may have shaped our self-esteem.

We've already mentioned confirmation bias, when we seek data that confirms existing beliefs. This bias makes it difficult to unlearn because we either actively or unconsciously tend to avoid exposure to perspectives that may challenge our own.

UNCERTAINTY IS HARDER

Unlearning involves moving into uncharted territory. This can be unsettling because we all crave comfort, and launching into unfamiliar terrain requires extra effort. And when that effort results in cognitive dissonance – new information conflicting with old beliefs – the mental discomfort can send you running back to your neural highway.

In fact, cognitive dissonance may be the leading cause of trader failure. It has often been said that the test of a first-rate intelligence is the ability to hold two opposing ideas in mind at the same time, while still maintaining the ability to function. But for many, having two conflicting thoughts at the same time leads to paralysis. Or worse: we ignore the dissonance and fall into old, familiar habits.

We resist new information and cling to old beliefs.

No matter how self-aware, we all have habits. Unlearning them requires changing established routines that are often deeply ingrained in the fabric of our daily lives. And acquiring new skills is time-consuming! In this age of social media, streaming platforms, and push technology claiming our attention 24 hours a day, it's easy to resist any activity that requires a substantial investment of time and effort.

Want another hurdle? We all overestimate our own knowledge and abilities. This overconfidence makes it hard to admit that what we learned in the past is outdated. Add peer pressure, social norms, and cultural expectations, and you can see why it's so difficult to unlearn behaviors of any sort.

Let alone habits related to profits. And loss.

> The first thing you have to know is yourself. A man who knows himself can step outside himself and watch his own reactions like an observer.
>
> **—Adam Smith**

CHAPTER SEVEN

UNLEARNING

For 30+ years I've maintained that the biggest mistake traders make is fading trend days – an observation I was first alerted to by J. Peter Steidlmayer when I sponsored his first book, *Markets & Market Logic*, in 1986. Shortly after a mutual friend brought us together, I realized the significance of Pete's observation.

Pete introduced me to the concept of placing time (a constant) on the horizontal axis, and price (a variable) on the vertical axis, so market activity can be organized under a distribution curve – enter the Market Profile. At the time, the concept of "market-generated information" was in its infancy.

After our first meeting, Pete left and headed toward the elevator. I'm grateful that he turned around, walked back into my office, and asked, "Would you like to sponsor my book?"

I asked, "How much?"

I handed him a check for $10,000, thus beginning my journey with the Market Profile and my love affair with market-generated information.

NOT FADE AWAY

My first memorable financial transaction was the purchase of a '49 Chevy. Observing my dad interact with auto dealers, I learned that the seller would offer a price to which my father would immediately respond with a lower bid – a logical response.

Applying similar learned logic as a trader can result in significant losses on downward-trend days. To be successful, traders must embrace a whole new logic that keys off the behavior of competitors, as revealed in developing market structure.

On downward-trend days, many traders can't resist the quest for an emotional high by attempting to buy the low for the day. When successful, it makes for great stories at cocktail hour. When this attempt is unsuccessful, however, they tend to immediately become sellers, which drives prices even lower. Then if they don't liquidate – because taking the loss is too emotionally upsetting – the financial risk skyrockets.

Ego gets in the way: "I'm right. Those other traders are stupid."

Upward trend days are the mirror image of this phenomenon. The ego trap of chasing tops and bottoms, for me, resulted in more than two decades of unprofitability.

Every time you fade a trend day, you're solidifying a detrimental chunk. That's where the real work begins if you want to increase the odds of becoming a profitable trader.

Fading trends is just one of the many habits you must change.

Knowledge emerges from the litter of our mistakes.

—Walt Whitman

THE CHALLENGE OF LEARNING AND TEACHING A MULTI-DIMENSIONAL SKILL

In his book, *Atomic Habits*, James Clear writes about the Goldilocks Rule, which states that "Humans experience peak motivation when working on tasks that are right on the edge of their current abilities. Not too hard. Not too easy."

Improvement in any endeavor requires a balance of stimulating challenges that push your limits and measurable progress that keeps you feeling engaged and capable.

When you're learning a new chunk (habit), it's important to keep the information as simple as possible. Otherwise, as the markets become more complex – or in Clear's words, "conditions aren't perfect" – you might find yourself seeking something simpler to do.

To add to the difficulty of this endeavor, most traders will be faced with the prospect of significant *unlearning* before they can advance on the path to competence, let alone profitability.

Each reader approaches this book from a different level of experience. For the novice, it may be hard to relate to some of these concepts. For example, until you have actually experienced the agony of exiting a trade far too early, or the ecstasy of pulling the trigger on a trade with an ideal location, it can be difficult to relate to the emotional nuances of trading.

For the more seasoned trader, on the other hand, it may be difficult to open your mind to new information, especially when it runs contrary to the chunks you've accumulated thus far.

Learning is layered. And in order to succeed, you must be aware of which layers you have and which you don't, as well as which layers you must peel away and discard.

The oft-quoted "five stages of learning" can help you better understand where you are on your quest to becoming an expert trader. It's important to note that individuals progress through these stages at different rates, and the process is not always linear.

1. **Unconscious incompetence:** Individuals are unaware of their lack of skill or knowledge in a particular area. They don't recognize the need to learn or improve because they don't understand their deficiencies.
2. **Conscious incompetence:** Individuals become aware of their lack of skill or knowledge. They recognize the need for learning, are conscious of their deficiencies, and begin to grasp the basics of what must be learned.
3. **Conscious competence:** Individuals acquire the necessary knowledge or skill, but need to consciously think about it – they can perform the task or apply the knowledge, but it requires focus, effort, and concentration. Competence is achieved, but it's not yet automatic or effortless.
4. **Unconscious competence:** Individuals have mastered the skill or knowledge to the point where it becomes second nature. The ability is now automatic, and individuals can perform the task or apply the knowledge without conscious effort or thought. Competence is ingrained and becomes a natural part of their abilities.
5. **Reflective competence:** Individuals not only perform the skill effectively but also reflect on their actions, seeking continuous improvement and refinement. This involves ongoing self-assessment and a commitment to lifelong learning.

It's not uncommon for me to read a technical book multiple times. During subsequent reads, I'm always amazed at what I missed the first time, as I was busy absorbing basic concepts. I encourage you to take copious notes as you read this book so you can begin to build actionable layers of understanding.

WE MUST FIRST AGREE TO TERMS

One of the obstacles to teaching trading (or anything) is defining a language that allows us to communicate complex concepts in a clear, concise fashion. The Market Profile is an effective starting point for introducing a common language for learning.

During this read, you'll be introduced to unique terms that evolved over my 50 years of observation and trading, such as poor highs and lows, pullback lows, and rally highs from trend days. (More on these in the ensuing Part II, "Fundamentals.")

Trading is a learning experience that never ends because the market is constantly changing. It's worth repeating: There is no finish line. The pursuit of trading success is a process with no end. Those who think they've "mastered the markets" will quickly find that change, as they say, is the only constant.

Because every brain has different strengths and weaknesses, we should each approach trading in a unique way. While there are common terms and patterns we can assess together, the moment of truth – when you place or close a trade – is yours alone, influenced by endlessly variable combinations of genetics, experience, environment, and emotion.

The level of difficulty is simply too high for most to stay with it. Many even fight the basic premise that *trading is not investing*. Effective trading is strongly dependent upon reading the actions of other traders, as well as understanding your own strengths and (more importantly) weaknesses.

It's useful to revisit Malcolm Gladwell's Diffusion Model, which can be very effective at helping traders identify the way human decisions are based on different timeframes:

1. Innovator
2. Early adopter
3. Early majority
4. Late majority
5. Laggards

You must assess where you are on this scale, and constantly seek to understand which of these timeframes are influencing market activity – which type of human behavior is affecting current behavior? Constantly seeking to find answers to these questions through unfolding, real-time market structure is the only way to have a shot at profitability.

GO SLOWLY AND BUILD A STRONG FOUNDATION

I'll say it again: Most traders set themselves up for failure from the very beginning, attempting to move forward too quickly, before they've got a handle on the multi-dimensional nature of this pursuit.

Successful trading can often be lonely. It's you against you, as much as it's you against the market. And when we're in a difficult place, emotionally, it's not always pleasant to repeatedly look inward in an ongoing attempt to assess whether or not we're perceiving market momentum without bias. Without fear or hope. Free from the influence of the subjective stories we tell ourselves as we navigate this fluid, often bewildering reality.

Patience is the most powerful ingredient for learning. Focusing on speed without precision never allows for a depth of understanding. When you begin to visualize developing market structure – seeing market action as more than constantly changing prices – you are on the right trajectory.

Beginning slowly lets you learn layer by layer, committing each layer to the subconscious, where it becomes ingrained and fuels your all-important intuition. Speed and precision come later.

Traders have a tendency to be seduced into believing that a single strategy will allow them to be competitive. But there is too much variability in the markets to rely on a single strategy. Especially one that relies on price alone.

Strategies come in and out of fashion, usually promoted by a trader in a chatroom, a pundit with hidden motives, or an "expert" on a book tour. My experience and observations over the years suggest that your highest odds of success occur when your strategy is consistent with who you are.

For example, I could never be a high-volume trader, executing five or more trades a day. This is something I learned about myself (painfully), and now I trade accordingly.

Before we dig into the fundamentals of understanding market structure, reflect on how often we tend to use tunnel vision. This occurs when we're predisposed to a specific answer, overly focused on order flow, or relying too heavily on specific references, to name a few common trader foibles.

When you become overly focused, the brain is wired to ignore information that runs contrary to what you're actively looking for – confirmation bias is a constant threat.

A famous example is the experiment where you're instructed to count how many times a basketball is dribbled, resulting in the vast majority of viewers missing the fact that a gorilla has waltzed across the court. You have instructed the brain to provide you with partial information, so you miss the big picture.

Don't let the gorilla take your money.

For the instruction that follows, we have narrowed our emphasis to short-term trading, which focuses heavily on day trading without restricting the holding period or timeframe.

Never lose sight of Hector. Less is often more.

PROFILE CHUNKING

The majority of the following Part II, "Fundamentals," focuses on chunking the Market Profile. To reiterate, the Profile is simply an effective way to structure and visualize the market's continuous, two-way auction process.

Step one will be to learn Profile nomenclature – the graphic's parts and their significance. Once this is engrained, so you can glance at a Profile graphic and automatically understand its components, we'll advance to chunking the concept of "value." We'll then advance to parsing different structures, such as trend days, rotational days, short covering, long liquidation, and so on.

The final section of the book will provide situational examples to make these concepts leap to life. Let's dig in…

PART II

FUNDAMENTALS

CHAPTER EIGHT

DEVELOPING DEPTH

Over the years, I have had countless conversations with traders interested in understanding market-generated information through the Market Profile. Occasionally these exchanges include the observation: "I'm a fast learner."

I don't recall any of these contacts becoming noticeable traders.

Earlier we discussed some of the cognitive biases that limit our potential. It's worth noting another one here, before we begin to study the nuts and bolts of the Market Profile – the Dunning – Kruger Effect is the tendency for people with a well-developed ability in one area to overestimate their competence in another area.

Consider a doctor who has dedicated decades to the study of the human body. Later in life they decide to become a trader, but enter the pursuit burdened with overconfidence, thinking their hard-earned medical expertise somehow translates to being a market expert.

I witness this costly assumption all the time.

The doctor forgets the rigorous, time-consuming, often tedious WORK that resulted in medical success. *And who wants to go through that rigamarole all over again?*

We humans are often extremely poor at evaluating probabilities, especially if our ego gets involved. This weakness manifests in poor decision-making while trading.

Looking back, I now realize how often I thought I couldn't *possibly* be wrong. More often than not, this assumption was roughly disproven. My intuition wasn't yet honed, and so it led me astray.

Honing intuition can challenge our naturally occurring belief that we can't be wrong. Our biases lead to tunnel vision, and we make decisions based on partial information, hunches, and ego.

It's hard to see our own flaws. Traders must develop safeguards against themselves.

> Our biggest weakness is not recognizing our own weakness.
> —**Shane Parrish,** *Entrepreneur, Best-selling Author, and Investor*

AIM FOR DEPTH PLUS BREADTH

As established, I endorse Josh Waitzkin's principle that *depth beats breadth every time*. However, when it comes to pursuing market mastery, I believe this statement is oversimplified.

Depth includes a mastery of nuances, and market nuances cover a broad range.

Years ago, while attending a NASCAR event in Fontana, California, I noticed my grandson was taking little interest in what he saw as "guys turning left all day." But when I began to explain some of the *nuances* of auto racing, his ears perked up. I explained that you can have the most powerful engine in the world (depth), but if you don't have everything else dialed in (breadth), you can't expect to compete at the highest level.

When do you come in for fuel? How do you tune a car for high humidity? What is the ideal tire pressure for the current roadway conditions? How well (or poorly) does the driver communicate with his pit crew?

When every car has the same monster engine, it is the *breadth of nuances* that decides who enters the winner's circle.

Before we delve into the nuances of trading, we'll first develop the depth of your knowledge of market structure using the Market Profile, a distribution curve that allows us to observe data in an organized fashion.

SUCCESSFUL TRADING IS CREATIVE PROBLEM-SOLVING

Creativity evolves from a deep understanding of the details that make up any field's foundation. To put this in perspective, reflect on what it takes to become any kind of professional – knowledge and experience must develop over many years, layer by layer by layer.

Detail matters. It's not until you have internalized the details of one layer that you're ready to move on to the next. And if you attempt to build on a poorly understood layer, the metaphor is obvious: you'll have a shaky foundation, and your whole trading approach can come tumbling down under live-market pressure.

Few appreciate the patience that is required to fully embrace this approach to learning.

The successful trader is able to recall important details, particularly when under stress. The recall of these details is what leads to effective creative solutions. Those less patient are unlikely to have incorporated vital details, rendering them oblivious to the ephemeral nature of developing market opportunities.

If you realistically approach learning to trade as a layered process, your chances will increase substantially.

Let's review some of the basic steps.

1. **Skill development:** It requires dedicated time and effort to develop your abilities. There will be continuous practice, training, and improvement. There are no shortcuts. Athletes train vigorously, musicians constantly rehearse, and surgeons must constantly seek to improve their craft.
2. **Survivorship bias:** Countless people have attempted to trade over the years. Only the best have survived, which makes the competition more difficult for new traders. In fact, what gives the novice a fighting chance is the continuous arrival of other novices. You need a strong competitive element to drive you forward.
3. **Commitment:** You must be willing to put in the time and effort required to excel, often at the expense of other activities and interests.
4. **Mental toughness:** The psychological aspect of trading is crucial – coping with being buffeted by shifting emotions and constant interruptions. Athletes, musicians, and skilled practitioners of all kinds must constantly deal with setbacks and self-doubt.
5. **Passion and drive:** An intrinsic motivation is present in all those who excel in individual endeavors. Those who succeed have a love for the activity itself, combined with a competitive spirit and appreciation for the work involved in becoming proficient – let alone an expert!

This layered learning approach is ever present as I write and mentor. I encourage you to take some time to examine the elements presented here, and consider whether or not you're ready, willing, and ultimately *driven* to embrace the rigorous, ongoing practice of balancing your emotions, knowledge, and focus in order to beat the odds.

MARKET UNDERSTANDING + SELF-UNDERSTANDING + STRATEGY = RESULTS

For the beginner, it's crucial to build a solid foundation rooted in the fundamentals of time, price, and volume. While developing this knowledge base, it's difficult to resist the allure of rushing to test your nascent understanding in the market, but that impatience to trade can actually hinder your progress toward a profitable career, ingraining bad habits you may not have even identified yet, let alone resolved.

The experienced trader, on the other hand, faces an even more daunting challenge. Like Hector the Collector, traders who have struggled to find success have accumulated a great pile of mental junk that feels like treasure, simply because it has been carried around for so long. This trader must confront the greatest obstacle of all: unlearning a mess of preconceived notions.

> Each of us has automatic habits. We have habits in movement. Habits in speech, thought, and perception. Habits in being ourselves. Some of them have been practiced every day since we were children. A pathway gets carved into the brain and becomes difficult to change. Most of these habits control us, beyond our decisions, to the point they function autonomously and automatically. When we stay open and pay close attention, it is possible to recognize these less helpful habits and soften their spell. And begin to explore new practices.
>
> —**Rick Rubin,** *The Creative Act: A Way of Being*

CHAPTER NINE

TIME AND SHORT-TERM TRADING

The first layer of information is often exciting and novel. And those delving into the first layer often seek to take each piece of new information and act on it, testing the fragment in the kiln of market activity.

As we have established, this is a mistake.

Experts who have mastered many layers see layer-one information as basic and nuanced – simply part of the foundation upon which they have layered countless additional observations, experiences, and insights.

As we delve into market-generated information, make sure you take time to appreciate the importance of *patience* in building your knowledge base. If you're able to build a solid foundation – which takes time and dedication to develop – you will eventually become a more agile, confident, creative problem-solver.

When the fundamentals are deeply ingrained, you can begin to recognize temporary market imbalances like a batter can read the seams on a slider. That's when you can make progress toward profitability.

> We always hope for the easy fix: the one simple change that will erase a problem in a stroke. But few things in life work this way. Instead, success requires making a hundred small steps go right—one after the other.
>
> —**Atul Gawande,** *Better: A Surgeon's Notes on Performance*

KNOW YOUR TIMEFRAME

If you are to become a successful short-term trader, you must first identify and address your biases – many of which you may not even realize you have.

The most relevant bias I've observed among short-term traders relates to separating *short-term trading* from *investing*. These two approaches are distinctly different when you break down the time horizon, objectives, and strategies related to each.

When traders fail to maintain vigilance around this distinction, they tend to focus on luck and wishful thinking, rather than clearly developing a challenging skill. They're also more susceptible to being whip-sawed by financial news that targets investors.

The standard definition says short-term traders aim to profit from short-term price movements ranging from seconds to months, while investors maintain time horizons that span years or even decades as they pursue value over time.

The primary execution mode at Jim Dalton Trading is *day timeframe*. But don't be misled by the word "day" in that context – our trades can extend for several days, depending on the developing opportunity and market movements. We don't trade in a vacuum; our process includes an ongoing assessment of the long, intermediate, and short timeframes, all of which must be considered as you assess real-time activity.

You can't profit from temporary market convolutions unless you understand when and how the various timeframes are interacting and influencing what you observe.

OBJECTIVES

Short-term traders attempt to capitalize on price fluctuations, regardless of the underlying assets' long-term prospects. They seek to generate quick profits by buying low and selling high, or selling high and buying low in the case of short selling.

Earlier, we addressed how "top-step traders" could occasionally benefit when the majority of short-term traders were literally *leaning the wrong way*. Your goal should be to focus on harnessing market-generated information to make a similar assessment when timing your buys and sells.

Organizing the market's continuous two-way auction process via the Market Profile is an invaluable tool in making this assessment.

Investors seek to build wealth over time. They're focused on the fundamentals of an asset, such as earnings potential, dividends, and growth prospects. Short-term traders seek to identify temporary imbalances when irrational human behavior – revealed in unfolding market structure – reveals short-term opportunities.

RISK AND VOLATILITY

Short-term trading can involve higher levels of risk and volatility. And short-term traders tend to use leveraged and advanced trading strategies to amplify potential returns, which increases emotional and financial risk – both of which can increase the odds of significant losses.

Investors focused on the long term accept market fluctuations, secure in their belief that their investments will appreciate over time; their risk tolerance is substantially lower than the comparatively frenetic behavior of short-term traders.

TRANSACTION COSTS

Frequent short-term trading usually leads to higher transaction costs that include brokerage fees and the spread between bid and offer, which can be a substantial hidden cost, as well as taxes if you're profitable. And if you're unprofitable, the yearly write-off is limited.

While short-term trading and investing are not mutually exclusive, we strongly suggest that they be carried out in different accounts at different brokerage firms. This will reduce the odds of long-term biases impacting short-term trading.

The unexamined long-term bias has undone many short-term traders' careers.

ANALYSIS

Investors typically focus on fundamental analysis, such as a company's financial health, competitive position, industry trends, and long-term growth prospects. Short-term traders are more concerned with market sentiment and price patterns, relying on technical analysis, charts, and short-term indicators to make quick decisions.

The Market Profile empowers traders to execute short-term decisions free of the weight and tangle of conflicting news, analysis, and scuttlebutt; it offers an unbiased look at the way price, time, and volume interact to provide vital clues.

> If you don't read the newspaper, you're uninformed. If you read the newspaper, you're misinformed.
>
> **—Mark Twain**

CHAPTER TEN

READING THE SIGNS AND FINDING VALUE

When you think about it, "trading" is core to everyone. We all make choices – *trading* one option for another – in everything we do.

It's challenging to teach trading because it's incredibly multidimensional, and there are multiple ways to address every cognitive challenge you'll encounter, with various sources of information, advice, and distraction. That's why it's so important to define a common language that enables communication about the essential components of trading. No matter how well I understand the market, I can't share that knowledge with you if I'm not able to communicate my experience in a way that *connects*.

The Market Profile and its simple, objective method of organizing information provide that common language. It enables me to translate 50 years of market observation and trading experience and give it to you.

Trading is a learning experience with constantly changing data and permutations. Again, there are many ways to approach trading, but in this book we have narrowed our focus to short-term trading, which focuses heavily on day trading without restricting the holding period or timeframe.

It's worth noting, however, that day-timeframe trading is relevant to all timeframes – no matter what your timeframe, whenever you enter or exit the market you're a day-timeframe trader.

SIGNS, EVERYWHERE THE SIGNS

It's December 10, 2023, as I'm writing this chapter. On *The Amazing Race*, an adventure reality game show in which teams seek objectives around the world, a father-and-son team is currently in third place. The father, a teaching assistant and football coach, is deaf. I find it amazing to watch the way he and his son communicate through sign language, even when one is driving, and the other is in the back seat.

"Signing" is also natural in music, conveying instructions like tempo and volume. Traders with an active imaginative mind will realize that the Market Profile provides "signs" that enable them to actively understand what the market is communicating. The "p"-shaped Profile in Figure 10.1, for example, signals short covering, while the "b"-shaped Profile in Figure 10.2 signals long liquidation.

Figure 10.1 "p"-Shaped Profile

```
              H
              H
          F   H I
          F   H I J
          F G H I J
          F G H I J K
        E F G H I J K L
        E F G H I J K L
        E F G H I J K L M
        E F G H I J K L M
      D E F G H I J K L M
      D E F G H I J K L M
      D E F G H I J K L M
      D E F G   I J K L M
  B C D E F G   I J   L M
  B C D E   G   I J   L M
  B C D E   G   I J   L M
  B C D E   G   I J
A B C D E   G   I J
A B C D     G     J
A B C D     G
A B C D
A B C D
A B C
A B C
A B C
A B C
A B
A B
A B
A B
A
A
A
A
A
A
A
A
```

EXPANDED PROFILE

```
H
H
FHI
FHIJ
FGHIJ
FGHIJK
EFGHIJKL
EFGHIJKL
EFGHIJKLM
EFGHIJKLM
DEFGHIJKLM
DEFGHIJKLM
DEFGHIJKLM
DEFGIJKLM
BCDEFGIJLM
BCDEGIJLM
BCDEGIJLM
BCDEGIJ
ABCDEGIJ
ABCDGJ
ABCDG
ABCD
ABCD
ABC
ABC
ABC
ABC
AB
AB
AB
AB
A
A
A
A
A
A
A
A
```

COLLAPSED PROFILE

Figure 10.2 "b"-Shaped Profile

```
A                                  A
A                                  A
A                                  A
A                                  A
A                                  A
A                                  A
A                                  A
A                                  A
A                                  A
A                                  A
A                                  A
A                                  A
A                                  A
A B                                AB
A B                                AB
A B                                AB
A B                                AB
A B                                AB
A B                                AB
A B                                AB
A B                                AB
A B C   E     H                    ABCEH
A B C   E     H                    ABCEH
A B C D E F   H I                  ABCDEFHI
A B C D E F   H I                  ABCDEFHI
A B C D E F G H I                  ABCDEFGHI
  B C D E F G H I                  BCDEFGHI
  B C D E F G H I J                BCDEFGHIJ
  B C D E F G H I J                BCDEFGHIJ
  B C D E F G H I J K              BCDEFGHIJK
  B C D E   G H I J K L            BCDEGHIJKL
  B C D E   G H I J K L            BCDEGHIJKL
  B C D E   G H I J K L M          BCDEGHIJKLM
  B C D E   G H I J K L M          BCDEGHIJKLM
  B C D     G   I J K L M          BCDGIJKLM
  B C D     G   I J K L M          BCDGIJKLM
  B C D     G   I J K L M          BCDGIJKLM
  B C D     G   I J K L M          BCDGIJKLM
    C           I J K L M          CIJKLM
    C           I J K L M          CIJKLM
    C             J K L M          CJKLM
    C             J K              CJK
                  J                J
                  J                J
```

As you learn to read the signs, you'll begin to associate short covering with a market that has gotten too short to trade any lower. When markets become too short, the short inventory provides temporary support because traders have to buy in order to cover their short positions.

The "p" shape is an indication that the buying was old business. (Traders were unwinding previous trades.) Had there been a more balanced combination of short covering and new-money buying, the Profile would have been more elongated. There's an old market adage: *Sometimes markets become too short to go any lower and must rally before they can break further.*

Conversely, a "b"-shaped Profile signals that the market has gotten too long to go any higher; an overabundance of overly enthusiastic buyers has accumulated too much inventory.

There's another adage in the market: *Sometimes markets must break before they can rally.* This is simply another way of communicating that inventory has gotten too long. Had there been more balanced selling (a healthier mix of old and new business), the Profile would have been more elongated.

The truncated Profiles in both examples communicate "old business." A one-dimensional look – a line of prices – would not have communicated the real context of the price moves.

Much learning does not teach understanding.

—**Heraclitus,** *Greek Philosopher*

MARKETS RUN ON INFORMATION

The three primary sources for market information are company fundamentals, economic fundamentals, and technical data. Historically, technical information has been price-based, but as we've established, price alone lacks *context*. The Market Profile provides that all-important context by incorporating *time* and *volume* – the fundamentals of any financial transaction.

To read and interpret the signs generated by those three components, the Profile organizes market-generated information under a distribution curve, just as scientists employ "bell curves" to study and interpret data. What is less recognized is that the *structure* of these distribution curves offers actionable insight into who is in control of current market activity.

The Market Profile allows us to visualize many complex patterns that result from the interaction of time, price, and volume. This visualization makes it easier to identify short covering, long liquidation, trend days, double distribution trend days, and relative balance, to name a few salient indicators.

A distribution curve compares a constant on the horizontal axis with a variable on the vertical axis. The brilliant observation by J. Peter Steidlmayer, a Stanford statistics major, was that *time* (a constant that's a component of any financial transaction) when placed on the horizontal access, allows *price* (a variable) to form the developing distribution curve of the Market Profile.

The Market Profile reveals signs that help market participants – continuously entering and exiting the market – better manage risk.

The Profile organizes information in the form of individual Time – Price Opportunities, or "TPOs." Every letter on the Profile is a TPO, starting with the letter "A" which represents the first 30-minute period after the market opens. This organization allows us to observe developing market structure, similar to the way you can look at the foundations of a house under construction and visualize what might eventually be built there; a small foundation is unlikely to become a skyscraper, and a large foundation won't result in a cozy cabin.

Figure 10.3 Example of POC Migration

START	9:30	10:00	10:30	11:00	11:30	12:00	12:30	1:00
END	10:00	10:30	11:00	11:30	12:00	12:30	1:00	1:30
PRICE	A	B	C	D	E	F	G	H
5108.00	A	A	A	A	A	A	A	A
5107.75	A	A	AC	AC	AC	AC	AC	AC
5107.50	A	AB	ABC	ABC	ABC	ABC	ABC	ABC
5107.25	A	AB	ABC	ABC	ABC	ABC	ABC	ABC
5107.00	A	AB	ABC	ABC	ABC	ABC	ABC	ABC
5106.75	A	AB	ABC	ABC	ABC	ABC	ABC	ABC
5106.50	**A**	**AB**	ABC	ABCD	ABCD	ABCD	ABCD	ABCD
5106.25	A	AB	**ABC**	**ABCD**	ABCDE	ABCDEF	ABCDEFG	ABCDEFG
5106.00	A	AB	ABC	ABCD	**ABCDE**	ABCDEF	ABCDEFG	ABCDEFG
5105.75	A	AB	ABC	ABCD	ABCDE	**ABCDEF**	**ABCDEFG**	ABCDEFG
5105.50	A	A	AC	ACD	ACDE	ACDEF	ACDEFG	**ACDEFGH**
5105.25	A	A	AC	ACD	ACDE	ACDEF	ACDEFG	ACDEFGH
5105.00	A	A	AC	ACD	ACDE	ACDEF	ACDEFG	ACDEFGH
5104.75			C	C	CE	CEF	CEFG	CEFGH
5104.50			C	C	CE	CEF	CEFG	CEFGH
5104.25					E	EF	EFG	EFGH
5104.00						F	FG	FGH
5103.75						F	F	FH
5103.50						F	F	FH
5103.25								H
5103.00								H

PRICE

TIME

At this point, begin to appreciate the importance of experience and imagination in getting an intuitive feel for what may be developing.

While the Profile in Figure 10.3 does not represent a completed day, it will give you a feel for how this particular day developed through the first eight 30-minute periods. Integral to this approach is identifying the Point of Control, or "POC," the fairest price at which business is being conducted. The POC is the longest line of TPOs closest to the center of the Profile's range.

In Figure 10.3, the bold element in each column represents the POC for that time period. As you will notice, the line gradually descends to the right through the first eight periods. The descending POC informs us that the fairest price is gradually moving lower.

You'll know you're gaining experience and becoming comfortable with the Profile when you begin to intuitively recognize the migration of the POC (either up or down). When POC movement begins to feel more natural, it's a sign that your intuition and imagination are working together to identify what is happening in the market in real time, in terms of *developing value.*

The POC is the starting point for calculating the Profile's "Value Area." Let's study the significance of this valuable indicator of market intention.

TIME REGULATES ALL FINANCIAL OPPORTUNITIES

In any financial transaction, there's a difference between *price* and *value.* Unless the price is fixed, the value is determined via negotiation. When we go to the supermarket, for example, we engage in a silent auction – we can either accept or reject the store's prices. When we reject an item's price, inventory accumulates on the shelf.

A more common negotiation occurs when we purchase a car. While occasionally we have to bid above the sticker price (prevalent during the pandemic amidst supply shortages), more commonly the sticker price is simply the starting point and we negotiate lower.

In stock and futures markets, price is determined via a continuous, two-way auction. Through this price-discovery process the market is attempting to discover *value.*

The heart of the Market Profile is the "Value Area," which represents approximately 70% (one standard deviation) of the Profile's daily range. The POC is the starting point for calculating the Value Area, which is an iterative process. First, count the total number of TPOs, including the single prints. Take 70% of this number to establish how many TPOs approximate 70% of the day's volume. Then examine the two prices above and below the longest line on the Profile, adding the two with the greater number of TPOs either above or below the original longest line. If the two lines above the fairest price include more TPOs than the two lines below the fairest price, you add the two lines above. If the two lines above are lower in count, then the lines are added below the POC. This iterative process continues until 70% of the TPOs are included (Figure 10.4).

Figure 10.4 Calculating the Value Area

PRICE	VOLUME	TPOs	SELECTION ORDER
5108.00	A		
5107.75	A		
5107.50	AL		
5107.25	AL		
5107.00	AL		
5106.75	AL		
5106.50	AL		
5106.25	AL		
5106.00	ACGKL	10	4
5105.75	ABCGK		
5105.50	ABCGHK	16	2
5105.25	ABCDEFGHIK		
5105.00 *	ABCDEFGHIJK	11	1
5104.75	BCDEFHIJK	16	3
5104.50	BCDEHIJ		
5104.25	BCDJ	4	5**
5104.00	BCD		
5103.75	BD		
5103.50	B		
5103.25	B		

* High TPO Price
** Only the closest price is used since it fulfilled the 70% or better volume requirement

Total TPO count is 78
70% of Total TPO count is 54.6 or 55
Value Area is 5104.25 to 5106.00

Once the Value Area is defined, we can begin to assess *existing* and *developing* relationships relative to value. Some examples: price and value could be identical; price could be above or below value; price could be positioned to return to value; or in a trending market, value could be in the process of moving toward price.

Price moves quickly, while value develops slowly. The artistry of trading is evident in this phase; successful traders exhibit their experience by remaining patient as value reveals itself amidst the froth and turmoil of changing prices. The art lies in separating constantly shifting price variations from the deeper clues of developing value.

If traders did nothing more than trade in the direction of the trend, or in the direction of developing value, they'd have a much better chance of success.

The importance of this statement is easily overlooked when emotions are surging and price volatility is high.

While the relationship between price and value is always relevant, it's only a single aspect of the Market Profile. The Profile also enables us to observe when prices are being made on increasing or decreasing volume, which is an important indicator we'll analyze throughout this section.

Our brains dedicate more space to vision than all of the other senses combined. That's one reason why the Profile is such a helpful tool in visualizing unfolding market information – it simplifies extraordinarily complex information in a way we can clearly *see*.

Figure 10.5 features a series of Profiles that enables you to visualize some of the day-to-day value relationships that provide important clues: overlapping value, overlapping-to-higher value, and clearly higher value.

As you gain experience, your imagination kicks in, assisting you in visualizing not only what is happening but also what is *likely* to happen. When you reach this stage, you're becoming a more creative trader, and successful trading is creative problem-solving.

Figure 10.5 Series of Profiles Showing Value Area Relationships

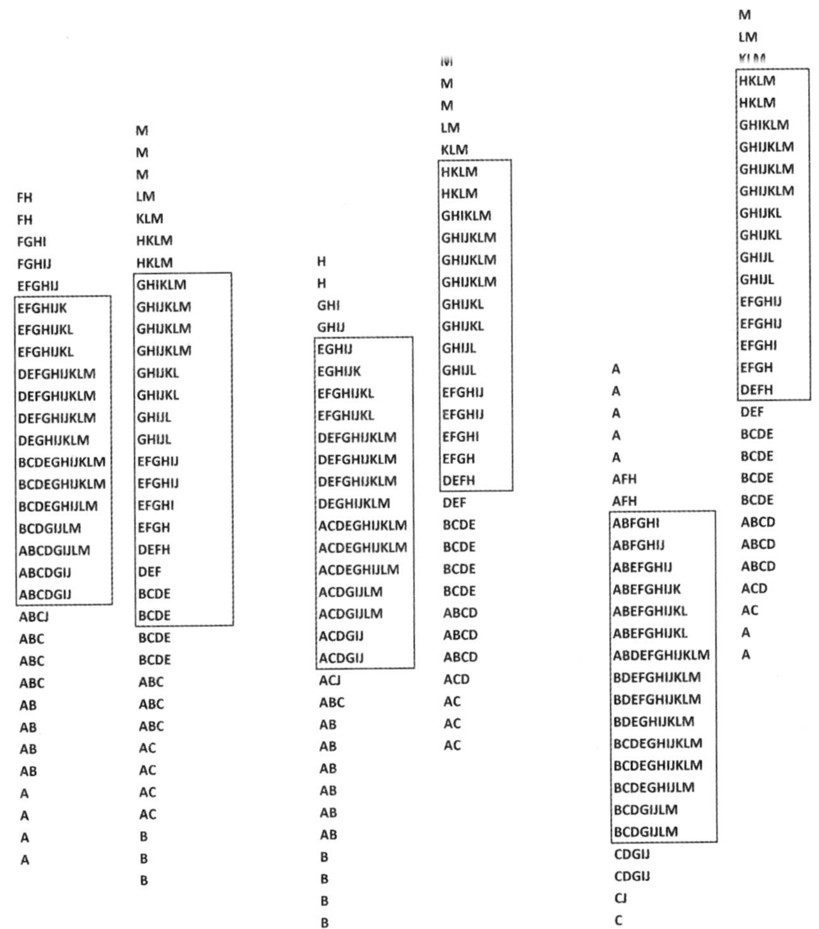

CHAPTER ELEVEN

BUILDING ON THE FOUNDATION

Consider again the analogy of a building's foundation to mentally prepare yourself to analyze the structural foundation of a market, as revealed in the Market Profile. Blueprints provide detailed, comprehensive plans for building a structure which only experienced professionals can interpret. This comparison will help you accept the training necessary to read and follow "market blueprints" in order to improve your odds of success.

Over the years, I have turned down many lucrative individual mentoring sessions. I've done so because I believe the individuals being mentored would not receive commensurate value. While I might be able to convey what is required to be a competent trader in a couple of weeks to a month, it's just not possible for anyone to assimilate the necessary information in such a short period of time.

How would you react to being offered a one-month course on how to become an expert surgeon, pro baseball player, or top-tier management consultant?

It seems simple: buy low and sell high or sell high and buy low – *what's so difficult?*

Trading, like any worthwhile pursuit, is a lifelong learning journey.

> The fact is that when there is intense competition, those who succeed have slightly more honed skills than the rest. It is rarely a mysterious technique that drives us to the top, but rather a profound mastery of what may well be a basic skill set. Depth beats breadth any day of the week, because it opens a channel for the intangible, unconscious, creative components of our hidden potential.
>
> —**Josh Waitzkin,** *The Art of Learning*

BEGINNING TO INTERPRET THE MARKET PROFILE BLUEPRINT

As a refresher, the Market Profile is a visual representation of the market's continuous, two-way auction process. Refer to the Figure 11.1 for the following discussion of a few critical indicators revealed in the Profile's evolving structure.

In the *buying tail* scenario, in A period, the first trading session of the day, price auctioned lower until buyers were discovered. Unless there are at least two single TPO prints, we don't define this activity as a "buying tail." The *lack* of a buying tail generally indicates that selling has dried-up, while a buying tail shows a more aggressive buyer response. The lack of a buying tail often indicates an unfinished auction, which produces higher odds of those price levels being revisited.

Figure 11.1 Components of the Profile

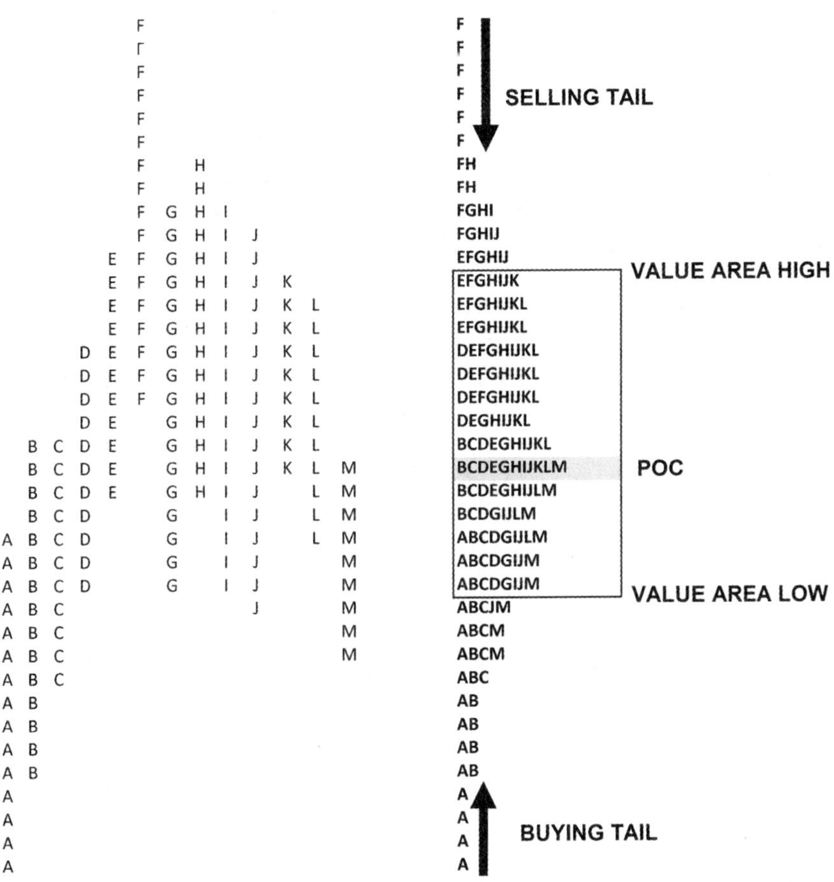

In the *selling tail* scenario, in F period, the market auctioned high enough to discover sellers. Had there been no selling tail, price would have simply auctioned high enough until the market ran out of buyers (bidders). No selling tail – similar to "no buying tail" – indicates the auction is probably not complete, increasing the odds that the high will be revisited.

Rather than simply attempting to memorize the definition of buying/selling tails, take a moment to reflect on the different reactions that can occur within the auction process. In A period, the auction could have simply stopped when the market ran out of sellers. As happened in Figure 11.1, lower prices attracted buyers, which is the most commonly expected reaction. A more aggressive response would have found lower prices bringing in more *selling*.

In F period, the market auctioned high enough to discover sellers, which is the expected response. In the mirror image relative to the buying tail, the buying could have simply dried up. Again, a more aggressive response would have been for higher prices to attract even more *buyers*.

Your goal is to learn to intuitively grasp whether lower/higher prices are bringing in *more* activity or *cutting off* activity.

POINT OF CONTROL AND VALUE AREA

We previously discussed the Point of Control (POC) as the fairest price at which business is being conducted (see Chapter 10). The POC is the focal point for determining *value*. A more dynamic appreciation, as you deepen your experience observing the development of the Market Profile, will enable you to estimate how the Value Area for a given day relates to the previous day: unchanged, higher, overlapping to higher, overlapping to lower, or lower.

The majority of traders focus solely on price. A smaller (though increasing) number of traders focus on value. A subset of those value traders have also learned to appreciate how value *shifts*.

Another reminder: Price moves quickly while value moves much more slowly. With experience, you'll begin to understand the conditions under which price will catch up with value, as well as when price has gotten ahead of itself and will return to value.

MARKET CONFIDENCE

In Figure 11.1, it's easy to observe that market confidence was fairly balanced. Early in the morning (A period), the market attempted to trade lower, and by F period the market was attempting to trade higher. The POC, which was at the center of the range by the end of the session, communicated that the day was relatively well balanced. In other words, overall confidence was evenly distributed between buyers and sellers.

Looking at a single Profile doesn't communicate realistic market conditions. However, our purpose here is to provide a "feel" for a single day. We will continue to develop a deeper understanding, layer by layer, as we proceed.

In my opinion, "day-timeframe market confidence" is the single most important factor for a day-timeframe trader (who starts with no position and goes home the same way). In the above example, the overall market confidence was evenly split between buyers and sellers. *Rotation* was the order of the day, with the POC roughly centered by day's end. There was no directional conviction and trading opportunities were limited. On a day like this, you're looking for opportunities around the Profile's edges.

We often enter a trading session reflecting on what we *think* will happen, what we *want* to happen, or (worse yet) what we *need* to happen. Learning to read and interpret the Profile and market confidence will tell you what is *actually* happening.

Survival is operating in the present tense.

A day with higher confidence will have a more elongated Profile, a POC that migrates in the direction of the auction, decreased rotation, and increased volume. While there are no good sources for volume, as a proxy we use New York Stock Exchange (NYSE) volume when trading equity indices, and futures volume when trading other contracts.

We classify a high-confidence day as a "trend day." One of the most frequently asked questions I get is, "How do I anticipate a trend day?"

The answer is: You don't. Rather, you read market confidence from the opening bell, and then you monitor for continuation.

THE DANGER OF BEING OVERLY FOCUSED ON LIMITED INFORMATION

My dad worked for the Illinois Bell telephone company for 37 years, first as a lineman and ending his career as a foreman. The single additional responsibility he had as a foreman was annual driver recertification.

The basic driving principle he taught me was how to remain focused on my total surroundings as I drove. This (literally) sweeping vision has stayed with me throughout my life. It goes like this: Looking straight ahead, your eyes shift to the rear-view mirror, followed by a check of the right-side mirror. Then you take in the peripheral view to the right, return to the rear-view mirror, then check the left-side mirror, finishing the circuit with a peripheral view to the left before returning your eyes to the road ahead.

Traders often become so fixated on a single view or price target that they don't consider other options or possibilities, even when they're plain as day to an objective observer. In layman's terms, we describe this as *tunnel vision*.

Part of the art of trading is assimilating how all the pieces fit together. As we will reiterate through this book, this kind of synthesis only occurs over time, and with considerable experience.

PREPARING FOR A DAY OF TRADING

As a brief illustration, I'll share my thought process as I prepared for the first trading day of 2024.

The most significant observation to make as you begin to trade is determining whether the market is *trending* or *balancing*. Every trader will have their own timeframe and perspective when it comes to this binary assessment – keep that in mind as I describe my preparation in the following example.

As the opening bell approached, my observation centered on discerning if the opening would be within or outside of the previous day's range. This is easy to determine, as electronic overnight trading occurs right up to the opening bell; one second the market is trading electronically and the next we're fully engaged in the day-timeframe session.

The closer the market opens toward the center of the previous day's range, the greater the odds that the market will be rotational, exhibiting early morning chop. Unless the market "single prints" from this range – exhibiting a high degree of confidence – I step aside until the market settles down. Engaging in this kind of early chop can be costly from two perspectives: first, actual losses combined with high transaction costs; and second, the expenditure of psychological capital.

Like financial capital, psychological capital is not unlimited.

Opening *outside* of the previous day's range increases the odds of an active trading session, as the market is indicating that it's out of short-term balance relative to the previous day. This type of situation offers two opportunities: failure to carry through quickly with a return to the previous day's range, or an upside/downside breakout.

When the market opens within the previous day's range, my focus immediately shifts to the concept of *developing value*. I observe where the market is exhibiting traction, manifest in the "thickening" portion of the Market Profile as TPOs stack up, revealing the area where buyers and sellers agree on value. My focus then remains on the dynamics of today's Value Area relative to yesterday's Value Area.

As you gain experience, imagination becomes increasingly powerful as you learn to visualize the most likely structural developments – will value be unchanged, overlapping, overlapping to higher, clearly higher, overlapping to lower, or lower?

Too many traders lack the imagination to assess the odds of developing value. Without igniting their creative imagination, they will always be late.

> Everything is a series of facts surrounded by other circumstances.
>
> **—J. Peter Steidlmayer**

More than just about any other insight, this Steidlmayer comment has driven my trading and teaching over the years. Let's attempt to enumerate a sampling of these "other circumstances," which will make or break you as a day or short-term trader.

Is Volume Increasing or Decreasing Relative to the Market's Direction?

Basic economic theory tells us that healthy advancing prices will attract higher volume. Higher prices on *declining* volume indicate decreasing odds of further advancement, and increasing odds of retracement. Likewise, decreasing prices that don't attract higher volume show lower odds of downside continuation, and increased odds of rebounding.

On the surface, this observation seems straightforward. But note that traders who recognize what's going on can sometimes act too early. As a general rule, you would ideally like to see the kind of "tail" described earlier prior to acting, as it provides more "surrounding circumstances" to support your trade decision.

There should be a totally different mindset between a trader exiting a trade and one who is entering a trade. The odds favor those who are a little early on the exit, and slightly late on the entry of a new position. These are important concepts that relate to emotional control.

Is Market Profile Structure Healthy or Unhealthy?

The relative "health" of a Profile can only be fully understood when you have gained sufficient experience. A healthy Profile is not too elongated, nor is it too truncated. Overly elongated structure suggests emotionally charged markets, and emotional decisions usually lead to poor results. A Profile that is too truncated shows a lack of interest, or counter-auction activity. Risk/reward in these stalled-out markets is not with you.

As you prepare for the trading day, always ask yourself what the market appears to be attempting to do, and what grade you would give its attempt. For example, if the trend is up and the market opens on the high and attempts to trade lower, producing a truncated Profile, that is a positive indicator for upward continuation, as it reveals that selling has most likely dried up.

And of course the inverse is true – if the trend is down and the market opens on the low but the Profile develops in a truncated fashion, buying has probably waned.

PRIORITIZING MARKET-GENERATED INFORMATION

One of the most ubiquitous questions during Jim Dalton Trading seminars is, "How do you prioritize this kind of information?"

While this is a logical question, it's unanswerable. Trading is an art, not a science. If short-term trading were a science, we wouldn't have a chance because high-speed computers would beat us to the trade every time.

Integrating the strategies discussed above is key to the process of becoming a trading artist; often it's the mixing and matching of individual pieces that result in the discovery of a trade opportunity. None of the elements discussed here are the same from day to day – thus you need an *artful* approach to remain objective, flexible, and focused on the details that matter.

It's worth reiterating, however, that the starting point for prioritizing market-generated information (MGI) is to determine whether the market is trending or lingering in an area of developing value.

LET THE TRADE COME TO YOU

One of the most confusing statements for many of our educational clients is "Let the trade come to you." Picture yourself standing at the plate awaiting a pitch that will rocket toward you at 90 miles an hour. Timing is everything – if you swing too early or too late, you'll end up in a pretzel punctuated by the THUMP of the ball in the catcher's mitt.

To be a successful trader, you must develop the patience to let the trade come to you. This statement is frequently challenged, as traders will say, "I'm looking for a trade, that's what I do." This statement may seem obvious, but it's incorrect.

When you have learned to observe and interpret MGI via the Market Profile, you'll begin to recognize when the trade has, in fact, *come to you.* There will be a confluence of factors that lead you to a nuanced understanding of what is happening in the present tense, who is in control of the dominant market impetus, and how the structure might develop over the remainder of the trading session.

When you go looking for a trade, you're likely to find one. Unfortunately, it's unlikely it will be a fortuitous trade. This is a difficult concept to internalize, and it probably won't register until the first time a trade appears without you looking for it.

MONITOR FOR CONTINUATION

Earlier, we identified two self-destructive habits: taking profits too soon and fading (going against) a trend day. The information that enables you to identify trade opportunities is the same information employed to monitor for *continuation.*

During this process, ask yourself in the case of a long trade:

- *Is value building higher?*
- *Are higher prices bringing in more or less activity?*
- *Is the Profile getting too elongated – a sign of emotional buying?*
- *Is the Profile like Goldilocks – just right?*

I'm often asked to share Profiles that demonstrate these (and other) scenarios. While this is a logical request, learning to trade simply doesn't work that way. The answers to the questions above only come from the experience of having witnessed the real-time development of thousands of Profiles.

Everything is a series of facts surrounded by other circumstances, and the other circumstances matter.

Monitoring for continuation reduces the odds of transacting too early or fading a trend day. Focus on the *process* for identifying trades, then monitor for continuation instead of dwelling on profit/loss.

Write down your unique process. Commit it to memory as part of forming a solid habit (chunk). Habits that change behavior are built one action at a time.

FEAR OF MISSING OUT (FOMO)

FOMO is a universal human tendency; we all want to feel like we're in the know, in the mix. While FOMO can be triggered at any time, it is most likely associated with:

1. Sharply rising prices in bull markets
2. Sharply falling prices in bear markets
3. Unexpected news events, for example, economic releases and earnings surprises
4. Short squeezes and liquidation events
5. Social media hype
6. Speculative front-running of economic releases

FOMO is a lot easier to write about than it is to control. But one of the keys to becoming a successful trader is developing an understanding of when you're susceptible to these feelings, and how they influence your trading tendencies.

KNOW YOUR COMPETITION

It's hard to imagine a competitive player entering a racquetball or tennis court without noting whether their partner is left- or right-handed. Successful trading is highly dependent on assessing the competition before entering a trade.

To be successful, you must know your competition, know yourself, and manage risk. For the short-term trader, I would place "know your competition" at the top of the list. This is an extremely complex undertaking. Over 50 years of trading, failing to acknowledge this has fueled biases that severely dented my profit potential.

The way to develop an understanding of your competition is to analyze the monthly, weekly, and daily bar chart, in that order.

It's extremely rare for markets to go directly from bull to bear, or bear to bull. The only exception that I recall revolved around the coronavirus that first surfaced in December 2019, sending the market sharply lower until March 2020, when the US strongly supported the market through fiscal and monetary policy.

The pattern you see in the monthly bar in Figure 11.2 represents what most often occurs – markets progress from trend to balance, then back to trend or reverse trend. "V" formations are extremely rare.

On the monthly bar chart the market clearly marches higher for several months. Don't fight trends. When the trend is up, for example, the odds favor orienting your trading to the long side. Take profits on rallies and look for opportunities to buy breaks. Don't outthink yourself.

Some of you might now be thinking, "He doesn't understand me – I'm a day trader."

So am I. The odds favor trading with the long-term trend.
It's not over until it's over.

—Yogi Berra

Figure 11.2 A Monthly Bar Chart

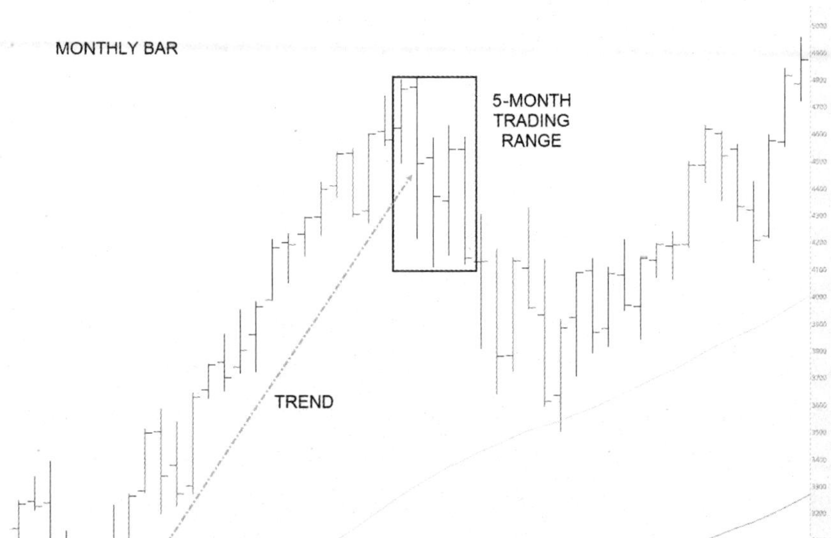

The weekly bar chart in Figure 11.3 shows a clear upward trend outlined by black arrows. The trend continues until there's upper excess, which is followed by a sharp, three-week liquidation break. This is a tradable short-term trend to the downside.

Reviewing the left-hand side of the weekly bar chart, which equates to the upper trend viewed on the monthly, you can easily see the effectiveness of staying with the trend by buying breaks and selling rallies (taking profits on rallies).

It looks so easy on the bar chart, yet we make it so hard as we become certain *it can't possibly go any higher*. The constant advice is: Don't defeat yourself.

Short-term auctions against the trend can be extremely enticing. They may be short-term profit-taking events, temporary responses to news or economic releases, rumors, etc. Remaining focused on the larger trend is

Figure 11.3 A Weekly Bar Chart

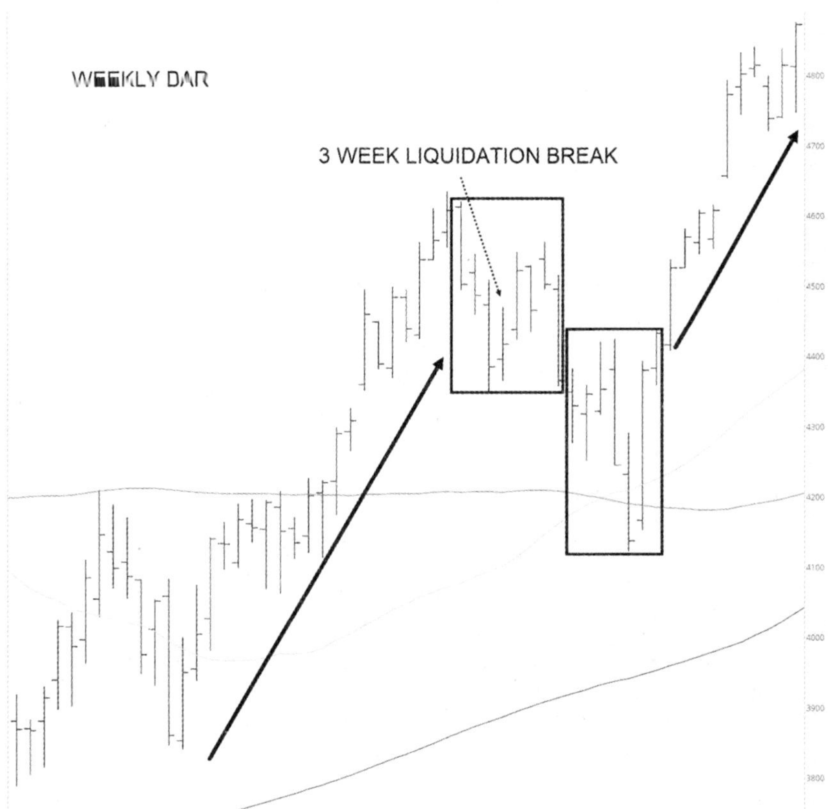

emotionally challenging, particularly following a day or days against the trend.

That's why daily preparation is so important. It's easy to promise that you'll consistently do the prep work, but promises don't prepare you for competition.

Substantial money is often lost in the late stages of a rally, as traders begin to front-run an expected break. While it's easy to suggest – and extremely difficult to execute – astute traders should strive to be a little *late* rather than a little *early* relative to the expected break. It's not uncommon for the earlier shorts (in this case) to miss the meaningful break as FOMO has done them prior to the downturn.

Unfortunately, most of us do not have an abundance of patience.

As we transition from the weekly to the daily bar chart, you should begin to see and feel the uncertainty, as a topping process is underway.

FIRST BREAK FROM TREND

It's extremely rare for markets to go from trending one way to trending in the reverse direction. Again, the odds greatly favor a transition from trend to *trading range*.

On the left-hand side of the daily bar chart in Figure 11.4, notice the first notable break from the upward trend. The odds are high that any initial break of this nature will be met with buying. Additionally, the first serious break is likely to be the start of the balancing process.

The buyers following the first notable break from an upward trend are most often "laggards," the weakest of market participants. Note that this "weak" label, while accurate, can create a mental block in your mind – late-buying laggards can often persist for longer than you imagine.

Learning and accepting this have been extremely costly for me over the years.

Your first defense is to recognize and accept the balancing process. Your ability to do this is directly related to your constant daily preparation. If you're not diligent, the markets will wear you down.

When markets enter this phase, I focus on short-term trends and balance; as a short-term trader, my minimum "balance" is revealed in two days of overlapping value. The more extensive the balance, the higher the odds of a more meaningful breakout.

Figure 11.4 A Daily Bar Chart

BALANCE TRADING GUIDELINES

As you are by now aware, I am vehemently against any hard and fast "trading rules," opting instead for a more fluid, context-driven approach to trading. That said, here are some of my personal guidelines that you might begin to incorporate into your own preparation and observational regimen:

1. Pass on trades that remain within a balance area, where chop is likely to remain high and opportunity low. Remaining within a balancing range serves to further establish and define that balance until the market determines its next directional move.
2. Go with any breakout from balance and monitor for continuation.
3. Fade (go against) any breakout that fails. The potential then arises to trade to the opposite extreme. As with any trade, monitoring for continuation is paramount, and will help guard against the inevitable surge of wishful thinking.

When volatility increases, the importance of *trading with developing value* increases sharply. If you don't focus on developing value, you're at greater risk of being constantly swayed and whipsawed by price. Trading with developing value isn't perfect; however, it is far better than hanging onto a flailing volatility rope.

It is not necessary to change. Survival is not mandatory.

—**W. Edwards Deming,** Economist and Writer

GAP TRADING GUIDELINES

As volatility increases, gaps become more common. While traditional technical analysis measures gaps from the settle, I believe it is important to only identify a gap when the market has opened outside the previous day's range.

You won't be surprised to learn that I don't define gaps by a specific number of ticks – there are small and large gaps, and as always, it is *the surrounding context* that makes the difference. The distinction will become more apparent through experience.

Here are some general guidelines I follow when it comes to gaps.

1. Go with gaps that aren't filled fairly quickly. (Frustrated that I have no precise definition for "fairly quickly"? All part of learning the art of trading.)
2. The best buying opportunity for an upward gap occurs on an attempt for price to fill the gap, when downward tempo slows and volume decreases.
3. If the gap is filled, begin to monitor for downward continuation. The ultimate upper gap failure would see, at a minimum, unchanged value.

Downward trading gap guidelines are of course a mirror image of these three points.

Successful gaps signal change; if the market has been balanced, a gap signals a change in the direction of the gap. The gap then becomes support for that shift. If the market has been trending, a gap may demonstrate acceleration of the current auction.

Larger gaps trigger more complexity:

1. Many traders don't trade overnight. So when a market opens sharply lower in the morning, for example, the lower opening is more likely to be exacerbated as these traders are forced to liquidate.
2. Broker-dealers servicing brokerage accounts with long positions on margin are likely to issue margin calls. Street wisdom says do not meet the call with cash but rather liquidate the position. As the broker-dealers liquidate positions, additional downward pressure is introduced.
3. As we have mentioned, momentum trading is the most recognized trading methodology. When a large downward gap occurs, the momentum indices are likely to be adjusted downward, which is likely to trigger additional selling.
4. If a large downward gap is to be filled, serious buying is usually evident from the opening bell.

MOMENTUM VS. MGI

The goal of the savvy trader is to discover the confluence of *momentum* and *MGI*. When there's a conflict between momentum and MGI, the odds initially favor momentum, because momentum is comparatively easy, and more likely to be the expected response from the trading hordes.

The expected response isn't necessarily wrong, but consider that the odds of an expected response are diminished when that response is not backed by objective information from the market itself. MGI, in this case, can be similar to a delayed reaction. For example, an upward move that is initially momentum-driven – but isn't supported by MGI (e.g. accompanied by healthy volume) – will most likely be limited, with higher odds of retracement.

When MGI and momentum are not in sync, the MGI reaction is often delayed compared to quick-trigger momentum trading – the heart of the issue for traders.

Today is January 11, 2024. On December 28, 2023, the market established a non-excess high at 4,840. My assessment was that while the market was continuing to rise coming into the end of 2023, traders were becoming skeptical of the advance; however, there was a strong hesitancy to take profits that would be taxable in 2023.

The first four trading days of 2024 saw the market trade sharply lower. I suspect the nervous longs that held out through 2023 immediately began taking profits on January 2, the first trading day of 2024. (Taxes were successfully moved to 2024.)

It's important to reflect on my assumption, which is that the selling that began on January 2 and ran through January 5 was primarily *liquidation*. This assumption is based on the lack of any meaningful downside follow-through (Figure 11.5).

Figure 11.5 Trading from December 28, 2023, to January 5, 2024

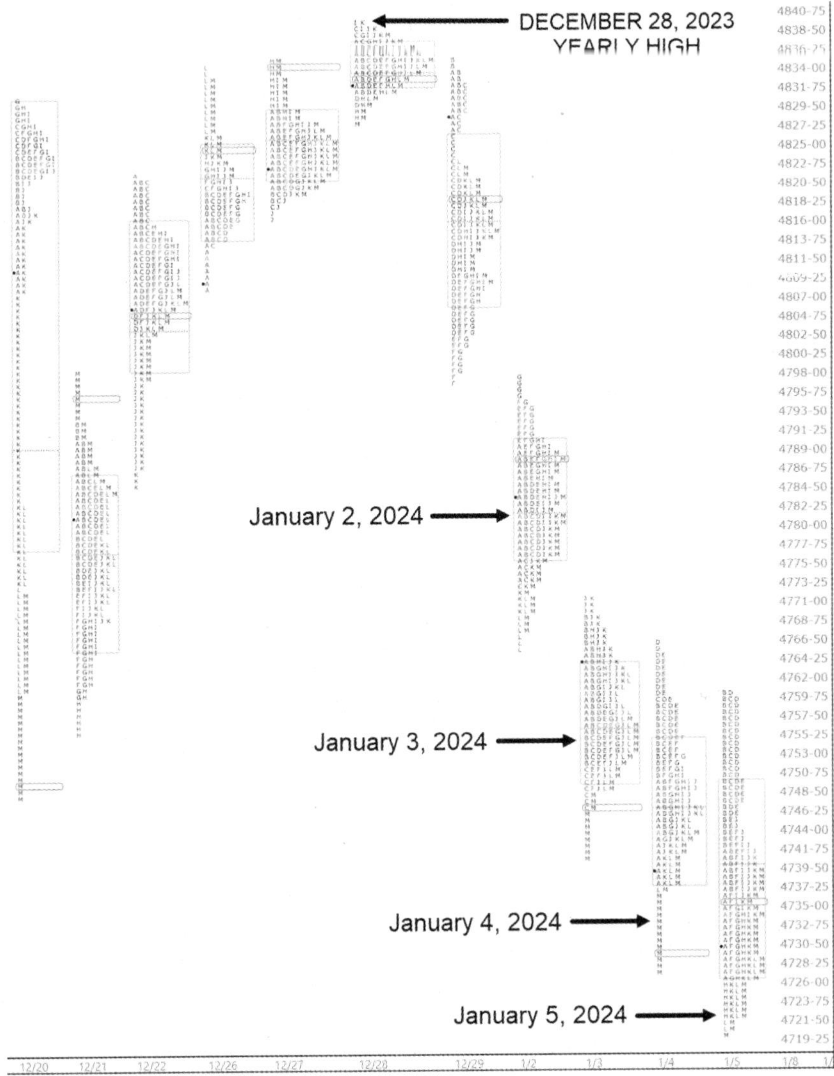

From January 8-10, the market rallied as momentum re-emerged (Figure 11.8). During this rally, many of the underlying references were weak, resting on exact reference points. When markets stop and start at precise reference points, it's often an indication that my competition is the very shortest timeframes.

Samples of some of these exacting references are previous highs, previous lows, overnight highs and lows, and halfback from overnight and the previous session. (This list is not all-inclusive, but provides tangible comfort for the discussion.)

As a trader, I felt the emotional struggles as the market continued to advance higher on these days. A casual look would be unlikely to identify the conflict, as "trend" and "value" were both advancing. The psychological battle taking place beneath the surface was that MGI was clashing with momentum; the Profile's thinness, reading from low to high, along with the four multiple distributions on the 8th (Figure 11.6), suggested that the selling from the first four trading days of 2024 had gotten short-term inventory too short.

This supports my earlier statement that the selling activity that began the first three trading days of the year was mostly *liquidation*. Here are two utterances attendees continually hear during my educational webinars: First, what happened before has a lot to do with what happens going forward; and second, short-term trading often revolves around inventory getting too long or too short.

Notice in Figure 11.7 that the Profile structure on the 9th resembles the letter "p," which indicates more short covering.

When inventory is too short, it can strengthen the market, but a short-covering rally that eliminates short inventory can weaken the market. Traders can sometimes get lost in the delay between the rally following a market that is too short and the break that follows a short-covering rally.

Figure 11.6 Multiple Distributions on January 8, 2024

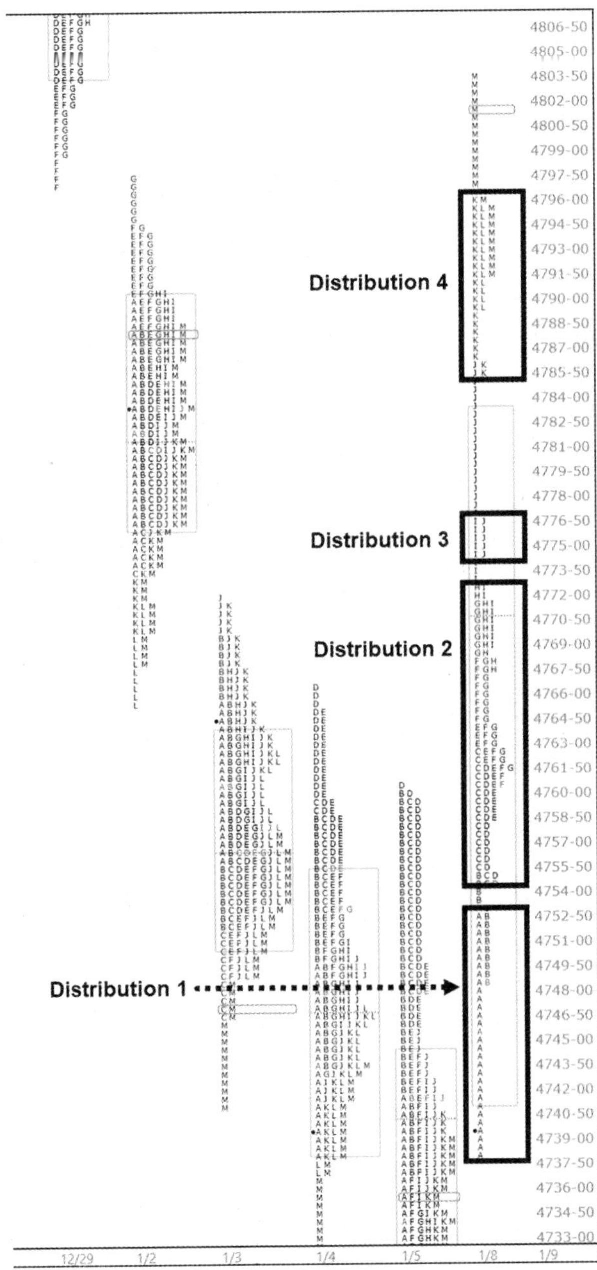

Figure 11.7 "p"-Shaped Profile on January 9, 2024

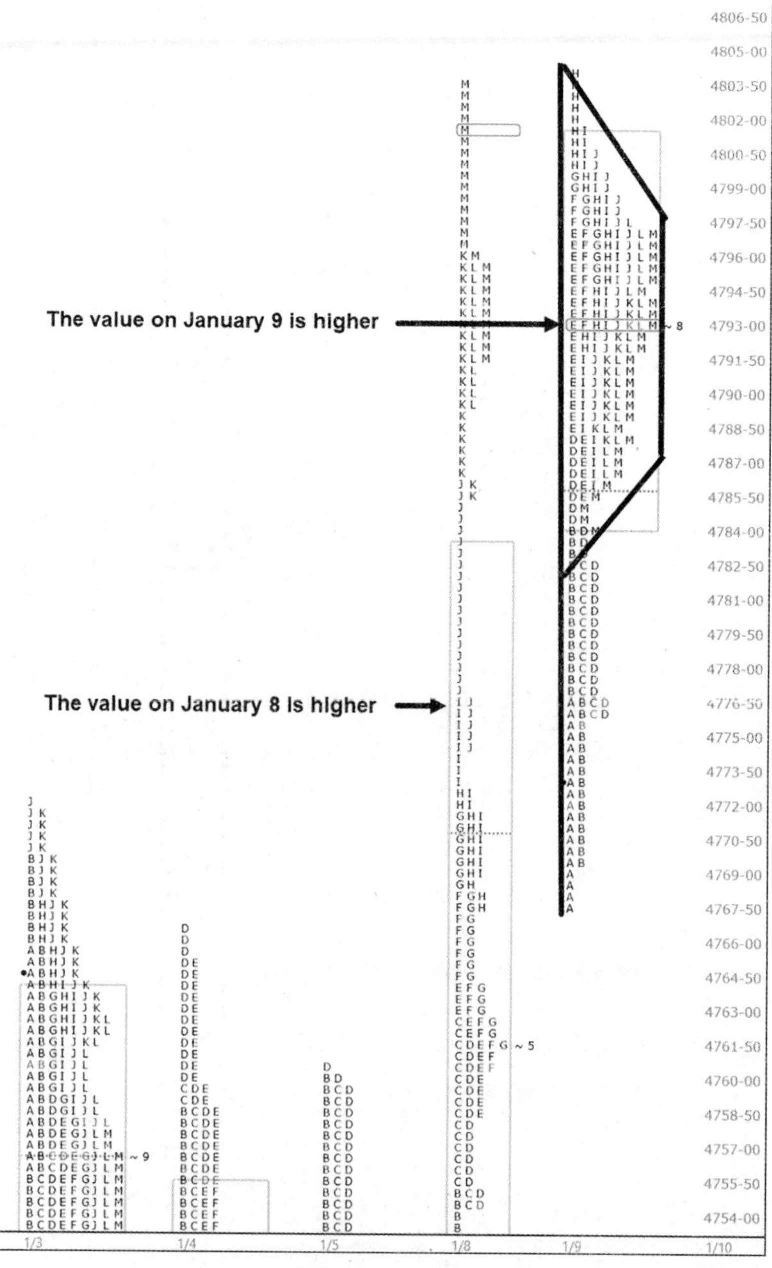

WEAK HIGHS AND LOWS

Weak highs and lows occur when the daily high is at one tick above, or one tick below the previous day's high or low. This is another indication that the current rally or break is not complete, which increases the odds of continuation.

Notice that the high on the 9th in Figure 11.8 fits this description.

Nuance matters. Weak highs and lows are constant nuances that adjust short-term odds for continuation. For example, a weak high followed by a sell-off has higher odds of not lasting. If not corrected today, carry that information forward.

> To acquire knowledge, one must study; but to acquire wisdom, one must observe.
>
> **—Marilyn vos Savant**

Following through on this scenario, we quickly saw that the weak high on the 9th was traded through to the upside on the 10th. This multiple-day rally appeared to be mostly short covering.

Supporting the statement "short-covering rallies can weaken the market," the 11th delivered a sharp retracement of previous days. Again, what has happened before greatly influences the outcome of what happens going forward.

Successful trading requires an organized mind that is capable of constantly reflecting on conflicting pieces of information. In most cases, the successful trader is capable of constantly thinking in terms of *probabilities.*

For example, the weak high on the 9th presented a probability that the market was going higher. At the same time, the short covering from the previous sessions increased the probability that the market would break.

Figure 11.8 The Weak High on January 9, 2024

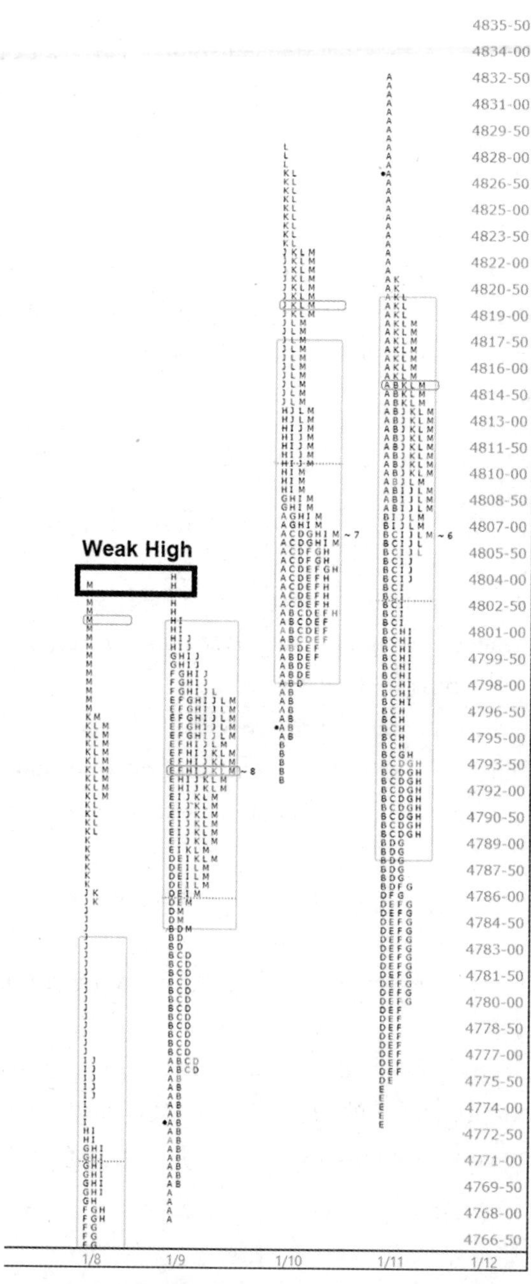

Hopefully this example helps you better appreciate the complexity, time, and life-long focus it takes to be a successful trader.

Take a moment to answer these questions:

1. Can you begin to feel the significance of MGI?
2. Can you feel the interplay between MGI and momentum?
3. What would you expect when both MGI and momentum are in sync?
4. What would you expect when they are working against each other?

CHAPTER TWELVE

TIMEFRAMES AND THE AUCTION PROCESS

Auctions enable price discovery, liquidity, and transparency. They create a competitive environment where buyers and sellers can seek fair prices – but "competitive environment" means different things, depending on your timeframe.

You can't fully appreciate the market's continuous, two-way auction process without first developing an understanding of the auction's participants.

The day-trader timeframe is minutes to hours, while the short-term trader operates over days and weeks. While all timeframes become day traders when they enter/exit the market, your sense of urgency depends on the duration of your focus.

Earlier, we described the "silent auction" you encounter at the grocery store, where you have a comfortable amount of time to make a decision. As a result, your emotional level is generally calm and controlled. Contrast this feeling with the amount of time you have to make a decision in the market's continuous, competitive auction.

The day trader is more likely to be impacted by such time limitations. During periods of high volatility, rapid changes in price can be extraordinarily challenging for day traders, who must be vigilant to avoid being swayed by extreme emotions.

I recall many moments in my trading past when I would peer down at my afternoon statement and wonder what the hell I just did.

Most day and short-term traders suffering unsatisfactory results are guilty of *overtrading*. In the digital age, entering and exiting positions are effortless, which makes overtrading – triggered by impulsive decisions fueled by emotions – much more common. Review your transaction costs under these circumstances. The commissions are visible, the loss of the spread between the bid and offer going in and the bid and offer going out are not as obvious. But they are real.

Continuous auctions facilitated the rise of algorithmic trading, which can quickly roll over day traders, especially following news releases, market breakouts, and events that result in a race to action. *The machines are faster and more consistent.*

On the other side of day traders moving in volatile herds are institutional investors and high-frequency traders benefitting from information asymmetry, obtaining and reacting to information quicker than short-term traders.

Day traders suffer the highest stress levels, for they must constantly monitor market conditions in order to make rapid trading decisions under pressure.

FACTORS AFFECTING PRICE

Sometimes price advances or declines are simply related to the competitive nature of other market participants. Fear of missing out (FOMO) is often behind these actions. As we quoted earlier, "Nothing draws a crowd quite like a crowd."

Sometimes psychology drives the auction process. Other times the market is feeling around a reference level, which can generate activity like "gunning for stops." It's not difficult to determine where a significant stop might be waiting – it could be a multi-day high or low, a trend line, a monthly high or low, weekly high or low, yearly high, etc.

For this example, let's assume the stops are above the current market at a monthly high. Experienced short-term traders intuitively know there will be activity there. These traders will bid (buy) the market in an attempt to trigger the stops. If they're successful – which turns the stops into buy orders – there's likely to be a quick rise. The short-term traders immediately sell into the market in advance to take their profit.

This is where you can continue to develop your intuition around market nuance: If the higher prices obtained by taking out stops fails to bring in new buying, the market is likely to retrace the move. As a day or short-term trader, if you didn't realize what was occurring, you could've gotten trapped on the wrong side of the market.

If trading above the reference level instead attracted new buyers, the advance would likely continue. Too often traders are afraid to miss a move and act too quickly.

Your best defense is awareness.

The odds of becoming a successful trader improve when you consider price action within the larger context of the market's continuous auction process, as well as the motivations of the other market participants. Know your enemy.

> In every discipline, the ability to be clearheaded, present, cool under fire is much of what separates the best from the mediocre. In competition, the dynamic is often painfully transparent. If one player is serenely present while the other is being ripped apart by internal issues, the outcome is already clear.
>
> —**Josh Waitzkin,** *The Art of Learning*

YOUR OPPONENTS' MOTIVATION

So far we've segmented market participants based on the timing of their actions, discussing general categories like Malcolm Gladwell's scale of laggards to innovators. Now let's look more closely at a broader range of participants, including commodity trading advisors (CTAs), private offices, hedge funds, large private traders, and investment managers (systematic traders will be included in this category, but systematic trading could come from any of these participants).

I'm writing this section on January 23, 2024. Last Friday, January 19th, the S&P E-mini rallied through both the 2023 and 2024 highs in spectacular fashion.

Let's discuss dynamics leading up to major references and potential breakout levels.

PRICE RISK AND LOCATION RISK

Many traders think of risk only in terms of *price*. This approach doesn't go far enough. Risk is also associated with key locations, such as a moving average, yearly high or low, anchored volume-weighted average price (VWAP), major trading range top/bottom, and so on. I'll be using an established trading range for the following discussion.

As a market approaches a major reference point, such as this yearly/bracket high, experienced traders recognize that it's a high-risk area – if the market fails to trade above the bracket. They may decide that the risk/reward is unattractive and exits before the market attempts to trade through the reference. If the trading-range high is exceeded, they will then re-enter their long position, believing the risk has been reduced.

Market breakouts such as we experienced in the E-mini S&P 500 futures contract (ES) last Friday, January 19, will often result in new orders above the reference/bracket high. When you look at the bar chart in Figure 12.1, this is very evident.

Figure 12.1 Daily Bar Chart from August 2023 to January 2024, Showing the 2023 High

But remember context – traders can be duped when volume slows as the reference point approaches. What can mislead you is that while the buying volume is light, which normally suggests the rally is failing, selling volume has also diminished, and without sellers the reference is much more vulnerable.

EXCESS

The two most important concepts I address in our educational seminars are *excess* and *balance* (covered later). "Excess" marks the end of one auction and the beginning of another. Excess is multi-timeframe. Most of the time our focus is on day-timeframe excess, which is expressed through either a buying or selling tail.

The graphic in Figure 12.2 shows a *lack of excess* for 2023. The significance of that became evident on January 19 when the market broke to new highs.

While this may seem obvious looking at a retroactive graphic, 14 days of trading took place prior to the market taking out the incomplete high. There's no rule that says the high must be taken out, but odds are good the market will eventually trade back through that level of apparent ambivalence.

The challenge for short-term traders is to keep track of this non-excess high while continuing to conduct their daily trading ("carrying information forward"). Thinking about it too much will make it difficult to complete your typical short-term trades. But if you forget about it, you might get caught off guard and end up quickly underwater.

This example is simple, as you're only tasked with carrying forward one piece of information. It's far more challenging when there are three or four (or a dozen) salient pieces of information to monitor and manage. That's where focused experience can lead to chunking, which reduces the amount of brainpower you must exert.

Figure 12.2 Lack of Excess in December 2023

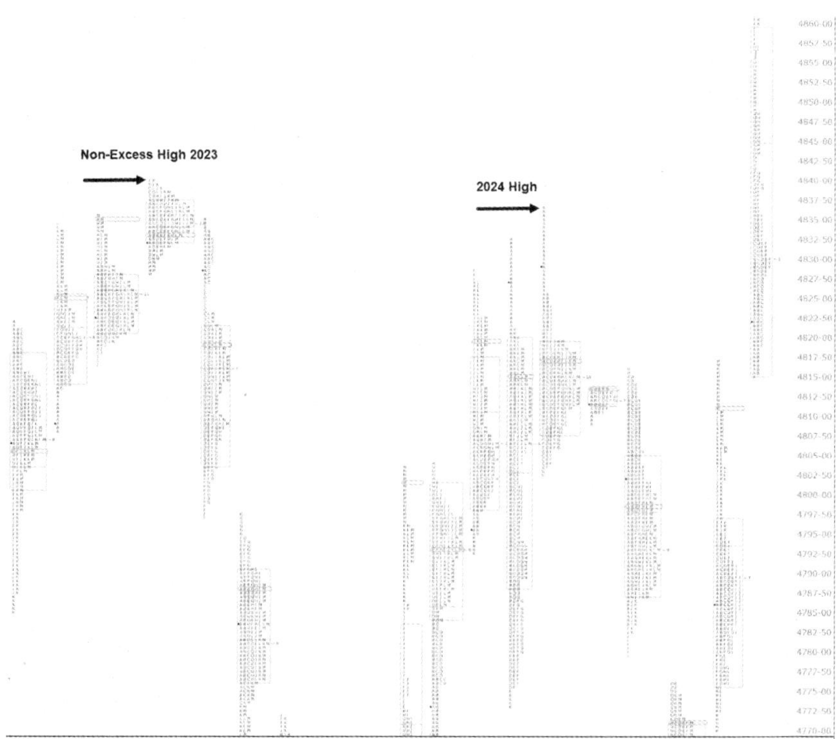

Most people would be surprised to discover that if you compare the thought process of a Grandmaster to that of an expert (a much weaker, but quite competent chess player), you will often find that the Grandmaster consciously looks at less, not more. That said, the chunks of information that have been put together in his mind allow him to see much more with much less conscious thought. So he is looking at very little and seeing quite a lot. This is the critical idea.

—**Josh Waitzkin,** *The Art of Learning*

CATALYST

What I'm about to share may sound oversimplified. In fact, when my trader friend first said it, I laughed it off: "*Traders do what works until it doesn't work anymore.*"

Reflect on how this philosophy might have contributed to the non-excess plateau that lasted for 14 days. From the December 2023 high until January 19, 2024, the market went nowhere. It appeared to be all short-term traders buying and selling within the confines of the established references, which contained the market for some time.

When markets get confined to relatively narrow trading ranges, it's not unusual for some kind of catalyst to trigger a breakout. The catalyst that took the market higher on January 19 was triggered by strong tech stock buy recommendations, further fueled by an overabundance of call positions that were due to expire and being hedged by dealers. Generally speaking, customers are long calls while dealers are short. If this is a correct assessment, dealers would have been forced to buy futures as the market rallied in order to maintain their hedges.

This isn't meant to introduce you to hedging, but rather to alert you to the fact that there are always many things going on beneath the surface – factors we don't know about until after the fact.

As you gain experience reading market-generated information, you will learn to read the signs that suggest these kinds of forcing actions are taking place. The lack of excess at the December 19 high was the first such sign.

CHAPTER THIRTEEN

TAKE A MINUTE TO BREATHE

You have made it this far – congratulations! Before we proceed, let's pause and seek a moment of calm… both to give your brain a break from processing complex information, and to make a vital point about how your mental state can influence your trading practice.

Breathing is a unique physical activity in that it obviously goes on throughout our lives without us having to think about it. But breathing can also be influenced by our immediate attention. Case in point: Join me in this simple exercise:

> Breathe in through your nose as deeply as you can, filling your belly fully, then breathe in *even a little more* to the point that your lungs feel completely filled. Now release all that air through your mouth in a giant sigh until your lungs are completely empty.
>
> Pause, and do that two more times.
>
> I'll wait…

Known as the "physiological sigh," this basic breathing exercise has many benefits:

- **Stress reduction:** Deep breathing activates the body's natural relaxation response by stimulating the parasympathetic nervous system, counteracting the "fight or flight" response and decreasing stress hormones (like cortisol) that trigger negative emotions, hindering your ability to remain calm and objective.
- **Oxygenation:** Deep breaths bring more oxygen into your bloodstream, promoting clearer thinking and reducing tension and anxiety in your body.
- **Muscle relaxation:** When stressed about a trade, you're most likely unconsciously tensing certain muscle groups. Deep breathing can help relax your muscles, reducing physical discomfort and promoting a sense of calm.
- **Focus and mindfulness:** Deep breaths also serve as a "mindfulness" technique, diverting attention from racing thoughts and illusory worries – the busy brain obsessing over negative outcomes that have little to no bearing on reality. Being mindful allows you to be more attuned to the present moment, where decisions happen.
- **Emotional regulation:** Deep breathing also helps regulate emotions, providing a welcome pause in a stressful or emotionally charged situation. Once you release unnecessary emotional energy, you have a better opportunity to collect your thoughts and respond to even taxing situations more clearly and calmly.
- **Reduced heart rate:** Deep breathing slows your heart rate. During periods of stress or anxiety – like when placing a trade – the heart tends to race, depriving you of the ability to stay serene and rational. A slower heart rate contributes to relaxation, which enables heightened awareness and better brain function.

- **Increased self-awareness:** Practicing deep breathing can help you become more attuned to your body's responses to stress, increasing self-awareness and improving your ability to manage stress effectively.

You know intuitively that anxiety causes shallow breathing patterns that deprive your brain of optimal fuel for processing new stimuli – you've felt it when you're about to pull the trigger on a trade when your heart races, you experience tunnel vision, and you fall back into unproductive habits and preconceived notions.

The deep inhalation and prolonged exhalation signal the body to shift from arousal to a more relaxed state of heightened awareness of the present moment – the only place we have any influence over ourselves and the world.

> In every discipline, the ability to be clearheaded, present, cool under fire is much of what separates the best from the mediocre.
>
> —**Josh Waitzkin,** *The Art of Learning*

CHAPTER FOURTEEN

TREND DAYS

I estimate that roughly 15% of days present some type of trend, with the other 85% being rotational. Here you might again be tempted to ask, "*How do I know if it will be a trend day?*"

You don't.

There are, however, nuanced clues provided by the market that can give you an indication of how likely a trend might be in play. The number-one clue is high confidence from the opening.

There are many forms of trend days, but let's begin with the type that is most likely behind the question above – the ultimate trend day that auctions unidirectionally from the opening. In the case of the day featured in the graphic in Figure 14.1, the market one-timeframed higher from the opening.

Keep in mind that this is an unlikely example, in that the market never demonstrated rotational trade, which can only take place if there is a cessation of one-timeframing. One-timeframing is only considered "over" when, in an upward trend, the market trades below the previous (30-minute) bar by two ticks. I have found that using shorter bars does not sufficiently provide the best market picture.

Figure 14.1 Trend Day

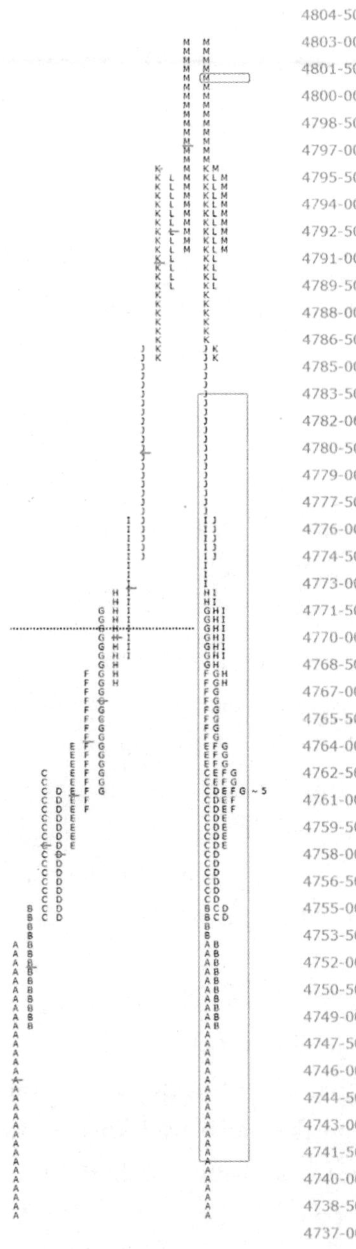

On the surface, this looks like an easy day to trade. However, many short-term traders – unless they get long early – continually ask the question, "*Where do I get long?*"

The answer is to get on the train and monitor for continuation.

Many traders, even if they get with the trend, exit too early. Additionally, they then *fade* the trend, enticed by higher prices in an upward trend and lower prices in a downward trend. Traders employing strategies that wait for confirmation are likely left at the starting blocks.

Some general rules of thumb, which of course must be considered within the larger context of surrounding activity, are:

- Don't fade a one-timeframing market.
- Don't anticipate a reversal.
- This is the perfect setup for *the revenge trade*, which happens when you miss a trend. After watching price go higher, you fade (go against) the move. You're psychologically attempting to prove the market wrong and you're right. This usually doubles your misery – you missed the trade, then you got stopped out going against the trend. In fact, this continual action by short-term traders provides additional fuel to force the market even higher.

I don't think I've ever conducted an educational webinar or seminar in which I didn't state that the biggest error short-term traders make is fading trend days. In upward trend days, inexperienced traders continually dream about selling the high.

This phenomenon can be even greater on downward trend days with continual attempts to buy the low. This thought was placed in my mind in the early 1970s by the manager of a retail trade desk. He actually announced, "The trade I just entered will be the talk of tonight's happy hour!" Which it would have been… if it had worked.

To be a profitable short-term trader, you need to capitalize on the big days. Reflect on the significance of what was just discussed, and your own tendency to respond emotionally to the feeling of missing a big move.

So much of what I've learned about trend days began with error. There is very little learning without error.

In my early trading years, as the market started to sell off late in the afternoon following an upward trend day, I would immediately sell into the break. A typical sale would occur as L period traded below K period (Figure 14.2), suggesting the cessation of one-timeframing. I suffered from an over-eagerness, as I had watched price rise all day. Disappointment would quickly set in as the market aggressively resumed its rally.

It's embarrassing to admit that it took years for me to realize the real market dynamics in play. The L period break was simply the market adjusting short-term inventory prior to its final run into the close. As you observe this formation, notice that the L period was the single period that the market stopped one-timeframing.

In the next example (Figure 14.3), we'll observe slightly different dynamics, when the cessation of one-timeframing occurs earlier in the trading session.

Observe the slightly different dynamics here. One-timeframing ceased briefly in D period. It's easy to forget this as the market continued higher for the next 2½ hours. The early cessation was a small clue that this market lacked the confidence of the prior example.

Second, notice that J period – two periods earlier than in the previous example – ceased one-timeframing again. It's another nuance that demonstrates reduced market strength.

The first example (Figure 14.2) produced higher odds of upward continuation than this day. In other words, the second example (Figure 14.3) produced higher odds of potential liquidation.

Trading is about change. Change offers opportunity.

Another observation I've made over the years focuses on the afternoon pullback low in an upward-trend day, and the afternoon rally high in a downward-trend day. If on the day following an upward-trend day price does not trade down below the afternoon pullback low, the odds of change are relatively low. Trading below the afternoon pullback low, combined

Figure 14.2 First Cessation of One-Timeframing

CESSATION OF ONE-TIMEFRAMING

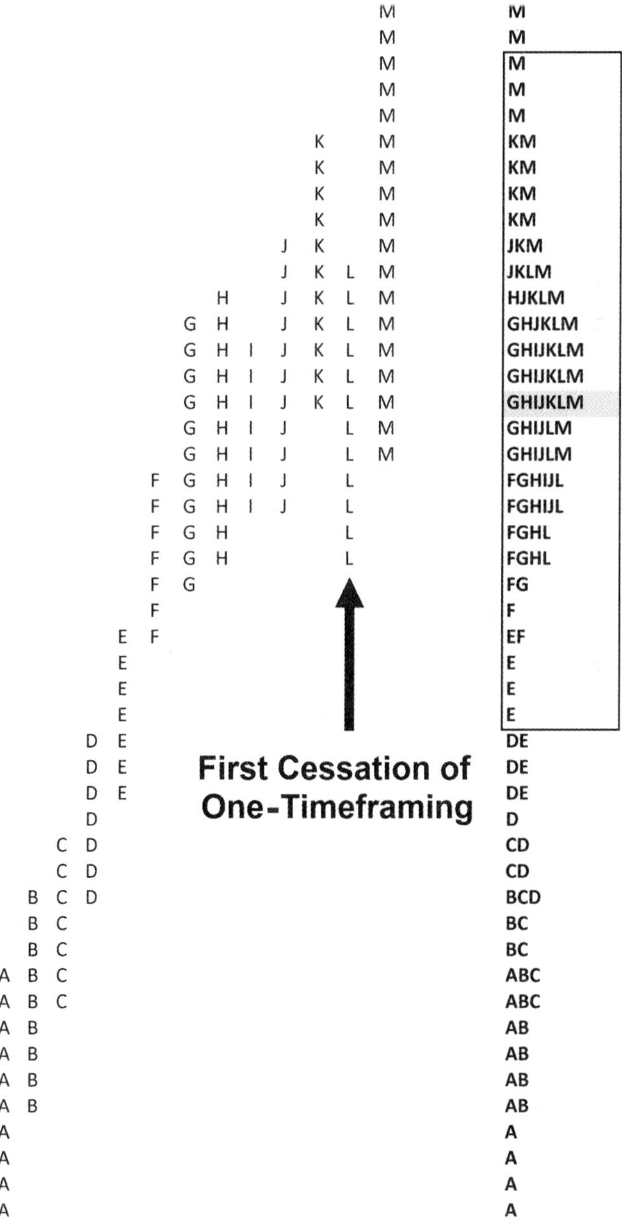

Figure 14.3 Second Cessation of One-Timeframing

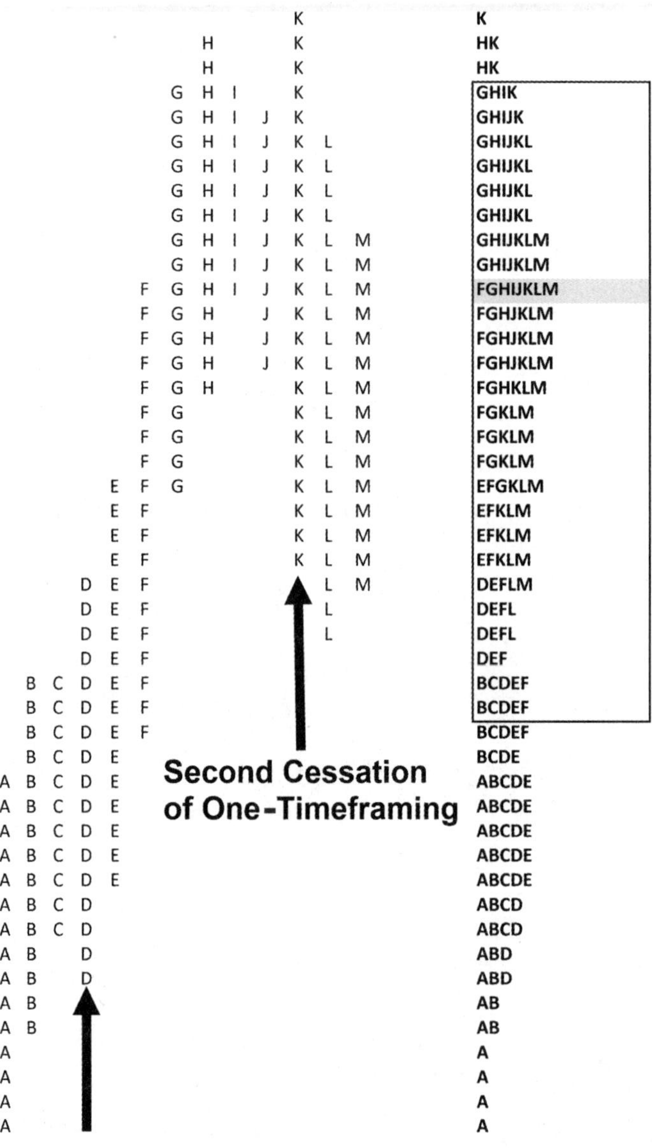

with acceptance, increases the odds of change occurring. Once again, it is the mirror image relative to a downward-trend day.

In an *attempted* trend day, pay close attention to one-timeframing, developing value, and volume in order to assess the strength or weakness of the attempted move.

NO POC ON TREND DAYS

The most frequently forgotten feature of a trend day is that you do *not* consider the point of control (POC) – or fairest price at which business is being conducted – while the market is one-timeframing. The nature of a trend day is the search for value, and of course the POC is the pivotal price for defining "value."

A failed trend day is the result of a day that initially began to trend, but then reverted to rotation. Once this occurs, the POC is again relevant. The failed trend day is now traded as you would trade any rotational day.

MARKETS ARE NOT ALWAYS ORDERLY

Sudden shifts in market sentiment, news events, and breaching key levels can all rapidly change markets. One-timeframing (trending) markets can suddenly revert to rotational activity, and rotational markets can just as rapidly transition to trending.

Relate this notion to our earlier discussion about how rising or declining prices can be the cause of further rises or declines. It's not uncommon for a rotational market to pierce an important price level, which sets off additional buying/selling that results in a "double distribution trend day."

Figure 14.4 Profile of a Double Distribution Trend Day

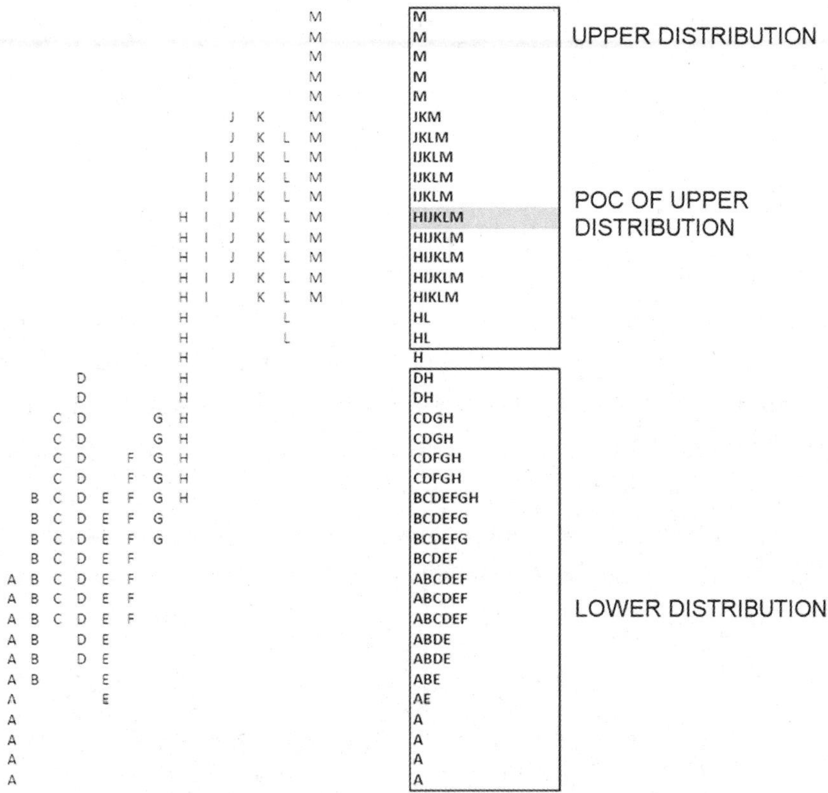

On the day shown in Figure 14.4, the market was rotational until buyers overwhelmed the lower distribution, spiking higher in H period. The separation between the two distributions (single prints) becomes short-term support. Once the double distribution is formed, treat each distribution as a separate day or auction.

The POC is tricky in this example, as it relates only to the upper distribution. It will be the longest line closest to the center of the range of the upper distribution.

Double distributions are normally the weakest of trend days. Only the final distribution is inspected to determine whether it is rotational or one-timeframing.

No matter what kind of trend day it is, it's still measured relative to the most recent value area. For example, notice if the trend day is higher relative to the previous day, unchanged, lower, etc. – it takes an artful interpretation.

Chunking is front and center again as you assess the overall effects of the trend day. Unless the day represents a clear upside or downside breakout, then the larger auction must be evaluated relative to all the interrelated pieces.

If I have any doubt about what the trend day represents, I go back and review the monthly, weekly, and daily bars. This allows me to view the trend day within a broader perspective. Context is king.

In Chapter 16, we'll spend time identifying and defining references and how they come about. Once we have a working grasp of references, we'll tackle rotational days, which make up approximately 85% of trading sessions.

MENTAL FLEXIBILITY AND TEMPO

Mental agility allows you to adjust to constantly changing market conditions, remaining objective and focused on the flow of market-generated information.

The example in Figure 14.5 presents you with what appears to be a trend day, but we will introduce "tempo," which signals that what happened earlier was simply a liquidation break – not a more potent combination of liquidation and new money selling. In other words, the new money selling was absent, which is a vital clue.

The constant refrain – *everything is a series of facts surrounded by other circumstances* – is again applicable.

The A period high is slightly below the high for the year. When the market starts to break in A period, you don't know if you're looking at predominantly serious new money selling, short-term liquidation, or a more serious combination of liquidation and new money selling.

Following the C period low, the market balances for the next two hours.

The market-generated information provided a feeling of "tempo." As in music, tempo can be fast or slow. In this case, tempo was sluggish. The frustration/challenge for many traders is that tempo can't be taught; it must be learned through experience. In this example, another way to view the dynamics of tempo is that offers were dwindling while bids were getting slightly more aggressive.

Traders that didn't understand tempo spent the next couple of hours selling every rally. Learning to appreciate tempo is a major factor in outperforming the herd.

Tempo is most powerful when it's married to *patience*.

One of the constant challenges we face as short-term traders is assessing if aggressive buying or selling is the result of liquidation, in the case of a market that was too long; short covering following a market move that resulted in the market getting too short; or "new money" buying or selling. Unless there is a panicked situation, serious new money selling is generally slower and more consistent. Serious new money sellers are holding many other securities, and it's not in their best interests to destroy the market. They will generally sell or buy in a controlled manner over a

Figure 14.5 Liquidation Break and Tempo

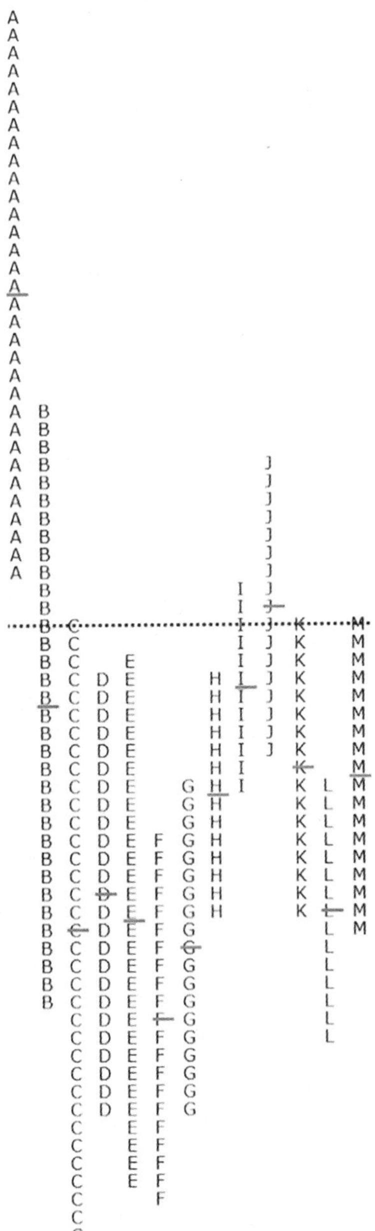

longer period – successful institutional participants will barely be noticeable. If they're impacting the market, they prefer it to be slow, gradual, and imperceptible. When prices are accelerating rapidly in either direction, the odds are higher that the move is related to short covering or long liquidation. Simply reflect on how you feel and act if you get caught long or short.

In the example in Figure 14.6, the market opened sharply lower following an extremely aggressive upward auction during the previous session. Overnight news had driven the market sharply lower by the opening. Here, the "facts surrounded by other circumstances" are that the trend is up and within striking distance of the yearly high.

Two short-term observations are in order. First, all auctions are pointing higher with the market within reach of the all-time high. Negative events and news announcements that are counter to the trend are most often retraced. Second, overnight inventory was short, and from the single A period prints, we know that overnight inventory was being rapidly corrected. About 75% of the time we will experience a counter-auction relative to overnight inventory.

NOTE: The earlier a potential trend day ceases one-timeframing, the greater the odds that the market will become rotational. As you know by now, there are no absolute definitions, but in the current example one-timeframing ceased in H period, which would be considered early. As we have observed so often, the market then became rotational.

Internalizing these observations will help keep your emotions in check during volatile trading sessions, which can make the difference between being whipsawed and experiencing a successful trading session.

Figure 14.6 Early Cessation of One-Timeframing

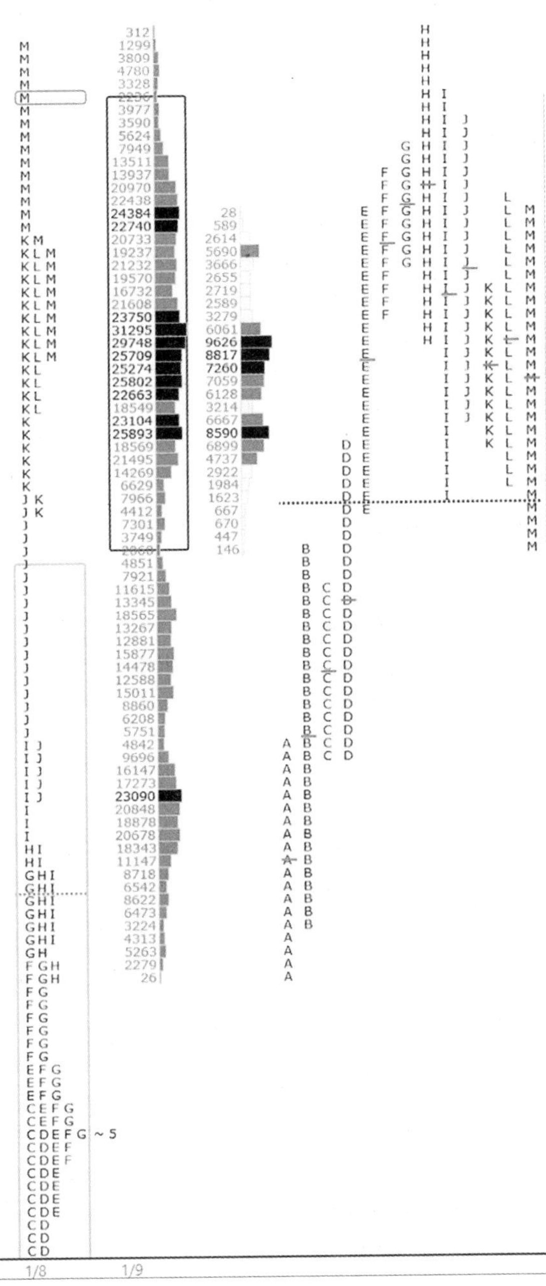

THE BUSINESS ASPECTS OF TRADING

Trading is a business: You acquire inventory, dispose of inventory, have a P&L, and are constantly operating within a two-sided market. Can you imagine having a small retail store with great inventory and no buyers?

This would not be a successful business.

The stock and futures markets are constantly searching for the area where two-sided trade can take place. When the market is one-timeframing, that search continues; when two-sided trade begins to occur, the search is over. This is the process that is occurring on a trend day.

GAPS AND SPIKES

Our definition of a "gap" does not conform to the typical technical definition, which measures from the settlement of the previous day to the opening of the following day. Our definition is much more dynamic: A gap only occurs if the market opens above or below – and remains above or below – the previous day's high or low. This definition is much more likely to signal significant change.

Our definition of a "spike" is a late price movement, either up or down, that occurs too late to determine if it was accepted or rejected (Figure 14.7). We employ these spike guidelines to help us manage this phenomenon.

In an upward spike:

- The base of the spike is support.
- Opening and remaining above the spike during the following session are positive, as this demonstrates that price had not advanced high enough to cut off buying or attract sellers.

Figure 14.7 Example of a Spike

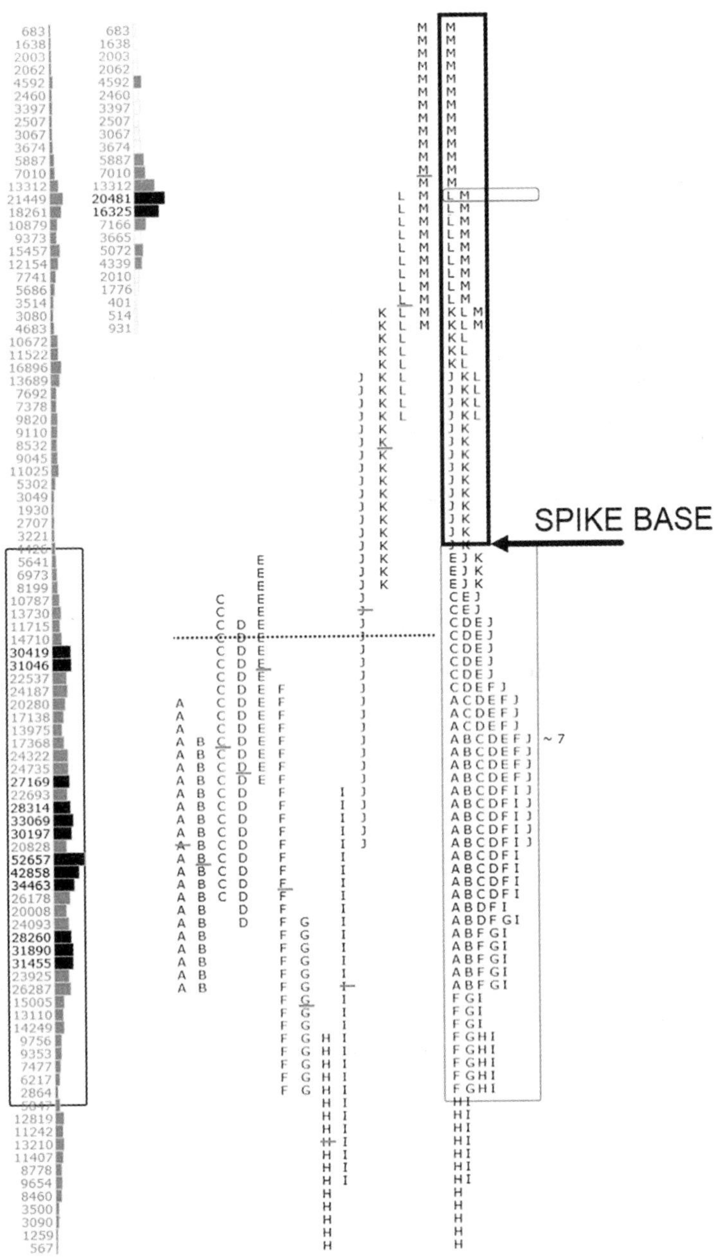

- Opening and remaining below the base of the spike during the following session are negative, as this demonstrates that price had gone high enough to not only cut off buying, but to aggressively attract sellers.
- Opening and remaining within the spike are positive, as this demonstrates acceptance of the price advance.
- A downward spike would be the mirror image.

Price is an advertising mechanism. We never know until after the fact the effect of this advertisement. It's important for traders to keep an open mind when reflecting on price.

- A manufacturer offers $10,000 off its truck's list price, which has gone too high to continue to attract sufficient buyers.
- During the pandemic, these same trucks were selling for thousands *above* list price – demand was high. Often, higher prices stimulate even more demand as clients believe the price rise is just beginning. In this case, the higher price was the cause of even higher prices.
- One client who owns a series of convenience stores with gas pumps told me that as price began to drop, he kept his gas tanks low and filled up often as he expected prices to continue to drop.

The reason for the discussion above is to expand your thinking about the way prices affect the market. In an upward trend day, the average day-timeframe trader has trouble resisting the urge to short the market. In a declining trend day, this same trader must fight the urge to go long.

A flexible mind will realize that sometimes the market sees the expected response, with higher prices attracting sellers. At other times, experienced traders will realize that higher prices are in fact causing *even higher* prices. In other words, the higher price becomes the cause for even higher prices.

Higher prices may lead to surpassing an anchor, such as the 200-day moving average, which in turn triggers more buyers. Additionally, higher prices could lead to even higher prices as shorts are squeezed and forced to buy to cover. As prices move higher, momentum indices are adjusted upward, which can trigger even more buying. You can easily imagine how this would also work relative to a downward trend.

Challenge your automatic responses unless they're well-honed. With an open mind, you increase the odds of determining if higher prices should be sold or bought. Too many of us automatically want to sell higher prices and buy lower prices.

I'm reminded of the parable of the blind men touching an elephant in different places. What each person feels shapes their perception: "*A snake?*", "*A tree trunk?*", "*A wall?*" This emphasizes the subjective nature of experience, and how our interpretations are influenced by individual biases and sensory input.

Mistakes are our greatest teachers.

—**Maurice Ashley,** *Chess Grandmaster*

CHAPTER FIFTEEN

EMOTIONS IN MOTION

Almost all of my critical trading mistakes have been related to the impact of emotions.

Emotions greatly influence the way we make decisions. I've taught trading for decades with constant references to this fact, but until this book I have remained on the surface, when a deeper dive was required. I have selected the discussion around trend days to attempt this "deeper dive," as I believe trend days present the kind of constant make-or-break opportunities that make it nearly impossible to trade from a calm, rational, clear-eyed point of view.

Emotions are complex psychological and physiological responses to stimuli that involve the activation of multiple regions of the brain. The following discussion is meant to provide a general understanding of these regions and what role they play in shaping your behavior.

1. **The amygdala** is often referred to as the emotional center of the brain, particularly related to fear and threat-related emotions. *How often do we hesitate because of a fear of loss, giving back profits, or simply being wrong?*
2. **The prefrontal cortex** helps with decision-making, impulse control, and understanding the contextual aspects of our emotions. *The vast majority of short-term traders fail, so to be successful, we must run counter to the herd.*
3. **The insula** is involved in many areas of emotional functioning, as well as self-awareness and the subjective experience of emotions, such as disgust and pain. *When we are wrong, we can become overly critical of ourselves or simply freeze; the disgust and pain magnify.*
4. **The hippocampus** is essential in forming and storing memories. It contributes to the emotional response by providing contextual information and linking past experiences to current emotions. *Many of my emotional/financial scars relate to decisions I made as a beginning trader. After a friend witnessed a particularly damaging decision, he commented, "I'm surprised you didn't bleed to death."*
5. **The anterior mid-cingulate cortex** is implicated in emotion, particularly related to emotional conflict and decision-making, because it's involved in linking reward and punishment information which elicit emotional responses. *It may sound obvious or pedantic, but this plays a major part in most of our conflicts.*
6. **The hypothalamus** is involved in regulating the autonomic nervous system, which controls physiological responses such as heart rate, breathing, and the release of stress hormones. *Chapter 13 on breathing provides a method that can have an immediate impact on this response to stress.*
7. **The basal ganglia** is responsible for handling complex processes that affect your entire body, such as motor learning, habit formation, motivation, and emotional processing. *As we continue to*

emphasize, you must first unlearn bad habits before you can form more productive patterns (chunks) of behavior.

There's a lot we know about the brain, but much more we've yet to discover. While you could spend a lifetime studying the brain, we know that *awareness* is a good place to start, in terms of learning to better understand how emotions affect your decision-making process. This kind of exploration can provide a road to recovery for those of us who are constantly torn between emotions and sound market observations.

Chapter 13 on breathing was intended to provide a simple method for calming your autonomic nervous system, which is always the first step in achieving a balanced, unconflicted mindset from which to trade.

EMOTIONAL AWARENESS

I've known many traders who are honest with everyone but themselves. Consider the fact that there might be a difference between who we want to be and who we are. Identifying your unique emotional awareness is a different process for everyone. This short list of practices will hopefully spark some ideas for developing your ability to retain a calm mindset when things get chaotic in the market.

1. **Meditate.** Meditation is a profound, challenging practice for developing a more comprehensive awareness of how your thoughts and emotions arise and disappear – and what we can control and what we cannot. While I've personally not found a meditation practice that works for my mind, I walk every day and either listen to books and podcasts, or simply perceive the passing sights and sounds as I quietly reflect on the day, my actions, and where I can improve. This activity gives my subconscious time to process and synthesize valuable insights.

2. **Journal.** Journaling helps develop a stronger awareness of how your thoughts and emotions are influenced by your daily life. What you're searching for are behavioral patterns that trigger non-productive behaviors. (More on this in Chapter 28 at the end of the book.)
3. **Read.** I'm a voracious reader of books and articles on the brain, the power of our subconscious mind, emotional intelligence, and self-awareness. The insights from the leading edge of the scientific community are fascinating and often revealing. In Appendix B, I recommend a range of books that have changed the way I perceive myself and the world.
4. **Practice self-compassion.** We all make mistakes. Recognize the difference between acknowledgment and self-criticism. Remember that the stories you tell – even if they're only to yourself in the private sanctity of your mind – have a strong influence on reality. Kindness goes a long way, both inside and out.

It should be noted that any one of these recommendations can be a lifelong pursuit, and as we have often stated: *Practice is the only path to success.* Developing a more nuanced awareness of your emotions, what triggers them, and how to cope with their inevitable influence on your nervous system is an ongoing process that requires patience, commitment, and your full attention.

Knowing yourself is the beginning of all wisdom.

—Aristotle

CHAPTER SIXTEEN

ANCHORS, REFERENCES, AND SUBCONSCIOUS BIAS

Daniel Kahneman, awarded the 2002 Nobel Prize for his work in behavioral economics, provides the foundation for the following discussion of references and anchors. Kahneman and his collaborator Amos Tversky are known for their work on "the anchoring effect," a cognitive bias in which people select a random reference point – then behave as if it's real and permanent.

The key is to *realize* when you're doing it, let it go, then get back to the market-generated information (MGI).

An anchor is any piece of information – no matter how arbitrary or irrelevant – that can unduly influence our judgment. These types of references can lead to biased trading decisions, cognitive dissonance, and emotional turmoil.

Here's a simple example: A retail item is marked $99.97 instead of an even $100.

You might think, "*Who are they trying to fool?*" But consider what goes on in your brain when you see a number that is clearly "smaller" than $100; we're not always aware of what our subconscious is doing, and as a result, we get swayed without realizing it.

The price tag $99.97 subtly *feels* better than $100.

Ancient brain circuitry releases reward chemicals that change our minds. Literally.

There is a danger known as "oversimplification bias," which relates to the kinds of references traders cling to. When we are solely focused on a reference point, it can distract us from perceiving the complexity of surrounding (and shifting) context – facts surrounded by other circumstances.

References can provide insight into who's in control of market behavior. But don't hang your hat on them.

RELATIONSHIP MANAGEMENT

Being a successful short-term trader means you've entered into an intimate relationship with the market. This can easily go astray. Relationship counselors are accustomed to hearing, "My partner doesn't listen," and "They just don't understand me."

Learning to listen to market references – while simultaneously considering those references within the context of unfolding market structure – will enhance your long-term relationship with the market.

THE RELEVANCE OF REFERENCES

We divide references into two categories: *static* references that will not change, and *dynamic* references that can continually evolve within the auction process.

Static References

The **previous day's settlement** is probably the most referenced – and the most emotionally charged – static reference. Simply observe market action when it is at or near the settle. Feel the search going on. Witness the way market participants are reacting to the reference: *Is there confidence or uncertainty?*

Another common reference is **last trade**, especially when it's significantly different than the settle. Both the settle and last trade are established by exchanges, and both indicators are watched closely by day-timeframe traders.

Next in order will usually be the **previous day's high and low** and **half-back**; any meaningful change will occur relative to these levels.

We have previously discussed **rally highs and pullback lows** on trend days, **gap highs and lows**, as well as references associated with **balance** and **spikes**. All can provide meaningful insights into who is in control of current market activity, and how likely it is that the activity will continue, revert, or remain uncertain and dormant for a while.

Other references include the **overnight high, low, and half-back**. And of course the **previous weekly, monthly, and yearly highs** are always relevant.

Our intention isn't to mechanically name static references, but rather to *wake up your imagination* to market-generated factors that provide nuanced clues to help you choose trade locations.

During our public webinars and educational seminars, we get constant inquiries related to "new money" buying or selling. There's never a perfect answer to these questions. However, the more the market is influenced by these exacting references, the less likely it is that meaningful new money is entering or exiting the market.

This is one of the most important concepts for day-timeframe traders to grasp and ponder. Day-timeframe dynamics are substantially different when the market is constrained by static references – versus days the market trades as if they don't exist.

The odds are much greater that something significant is occurring when there is only minimal hesitation at these references.

Dynamic References

Dynamic references change in relationship to market activity. For example, during an upward-trend day, the high will constantly change. Additionally, you may experience new weekly, monthly, quarterly highs, etc.

During days that are more rotational in nature, the evolving Point of Control (POC) can be very informational. As a refresher, the POC is the fairest price at which business is being conducted. During a session in which value is developing higher, for example, a POC that constantly migrates higher indicates a healthy advance and increases the odds of continuation. A less robust POC indicates less upward enthusiasm – which doesn't necessarily mean there will be a reversal or retrenchment, but the odds of giveback are higher.

Does *monitoring for continuation* come to mind?

DAY-TIMEFRAME TRADING AND REFERENCES

The graphic in Figure 16.1 was captured prior to the opening on Monday, February 5, 2024. It reveals the behavior of overnight traders, who are generally the weakest of short-term traders.

The overnight high is within two ticks of Friday's settle, with the overnight low at Friday's half-back. The market communicates, but if you're lost in focus bias you may miss this important bit of information.

Relationship counseling may be in order: "*He just doesn't listen.*"

Being inside Friday's range with an almost exacting high and low tells me the market is neutral relative to Friday; no longer-term money has yet shown interest. Additionally, the market is likely to open within Friday's range – another indication that there is no obvious change in prevailing conditions.

Too often traders become emotionally charged waiting for the opening. In that overcharged state, the odds are high that your decisions will not be objective.

For example, I was once chatting with a long-term client before the market's opening. He commented that I was sitting back, taking "a landscape view" of the market as we waited.

I asked, "What do you do?"

He replied, "I'm hunched up close to the screen to observe the opening."

Having put this thought in my mind, I began to observe other traders as the opening approached – my friend was closer to the norm: too emotionally involved, which puts you on the wrong foot to start the day.

This anecdote is meant to demonstrate the way these types of references can assist you and guide your day-timeframe trading.

If you're able to listen...

Figure 16.1 Overnight Trade, Before Opening, Monday, February 5, 2024

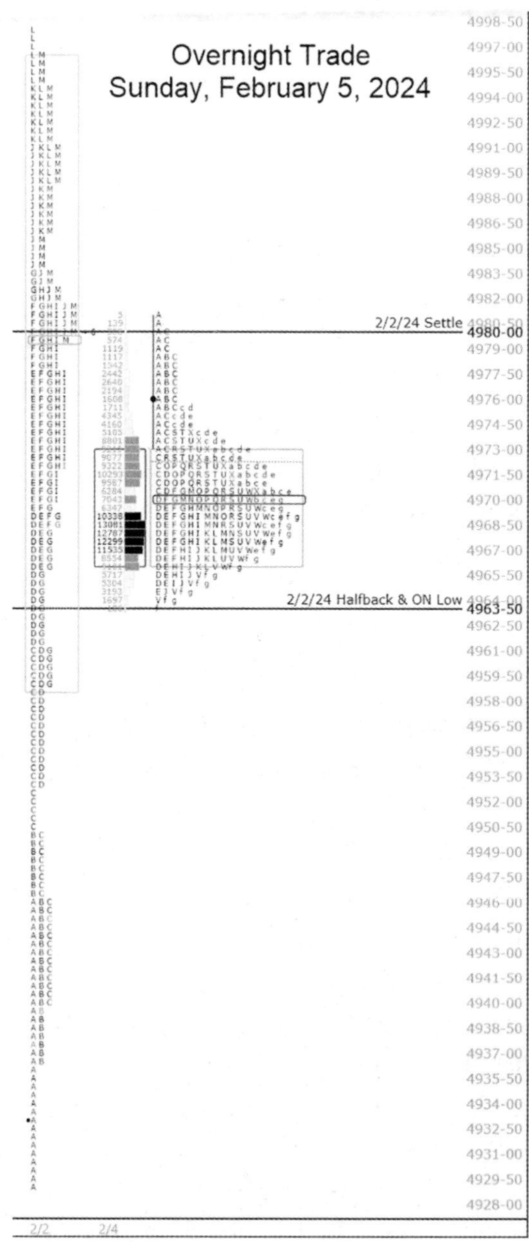

CHAPTER SEVENTEEN

PRIORITIZING REFERENCES

I'm constantly asked to *prioritize references*. This request appears to be simple and logical, but it's actually nuanced and complex. My first employment of references is to determine who is controlling the majority of day-timeframe trading. When the market is constantly being contained by easily identifiable references, the odds are high that trading on that day is mostly being conducted by short-term, day-timeframe traders.

Easily identifiable references would include the previous day's high or low, the settle, half-back from the previous day, overnight high/low, etc.

When the market plows right through easily identifiable references, it's an indication that one of the below is occurring:

- Longer timeframes are active
- Short covering
- Long liquidation
- Combination of all three

When my mind is open and free of bias, these types of observations greatly influence my trading. The market no longer has occasion to complain, "*He never listens.*"

Pay close attention to this nuance: When the market is being influenced by day-timeframe traders, you're far more likely to witness constant support and resistance taking place at half-back relative to the prior or current 30-minute period. When the market is ignoring these nuanced references, it's more likely that longer timeframes are active. The graphic in Figure 17.1 allows you to observe that on this sharply declining day, there is no unusual activity around the half-back from the prior 30-minute period; longer-timeframe sellers are active. It could be long liquidation, new money selling, or a combination of the two. More information is required to make this determination.

As always, *monitor for continuation.*

Orienting your trading strategy with an acute awareness of how the market is responding to reference points is an important step toward successful trading. Without this awareness, it's far more difficult to remain oriented to what's actually occurring, and you're more likely to get whip-sawed.

NOT ALL REFERENCES ARE CREATED EQUAL

Earlier we wrote that higher prices may be the cause of *even higher* prices (and of course the opposite for lower prices). Higher prices may lead to breakouts above bracket highs, yearly highs, etc. – a common occurrence, and as traders, we deal with it every day.

What is more likely to catch you off-guard is the entry of systematic or computer-based programs executed by commodity trading advisors, hedge

Figure 17.1 Example of a Market Not Influenced by Day-Timeframe Traders

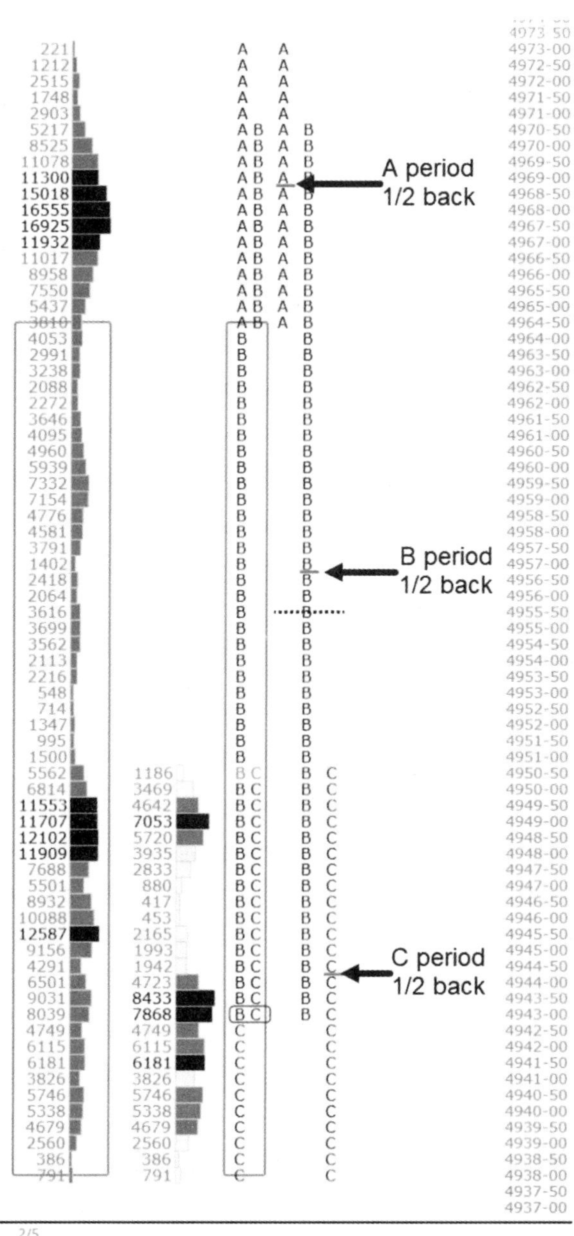

funds, family offices, etc. These programs are most likely to occur under one of these conditions:

- Markets searching for a low
- Markets searching for a high
- Trend continuation or acceleration

I find them most potent when associated with trend continuation, a market action that is more likely to catch me off-guard; they're often sudden and unexpected.

While I don't have access to these programs, I suspect they're driven by price-based, quantitative algorithms.

These algorithms often have a trigger-point execution; I have observed that these trades frequently begin at exacting references, such as a prior daily high/low, half-back relative to the current day's trading (relative to the entire day, not the 30-minute bar), the settle, etc. Once these programs are underway, they can continue for days.

Figure 17.2 is a partial Profile that depicts the day-timeframe references that occur when the shortest timeframes gain control. One of the primary challenges of being a day-timeframe trader is *other day-timeframe traders*, most of whom only know how to click "buy" and "sell," react to visible references, and chase momentum.

By learning to observe references, you greatly increase your chances of knowing who is your actual competition in real time. This doesn't assure a win, obviously, but it will certainly increase your odds of success.

Finally, when addressing references, you should create a tracking system. It's difficult and often confusing to keep a complete list of short-term references in mind. And it might seem simple to remember round numbers (4,000, 5,000, etc.), but other, more nuanced references can become more obscure and difficult to monitor over time.

Regarding older references, I'm fond of the phrase, "carrying information forward." The trick is to set those references aside that aren't likely to

Figure 17.2 Example of a Market in Control of the Shortest Timeframe

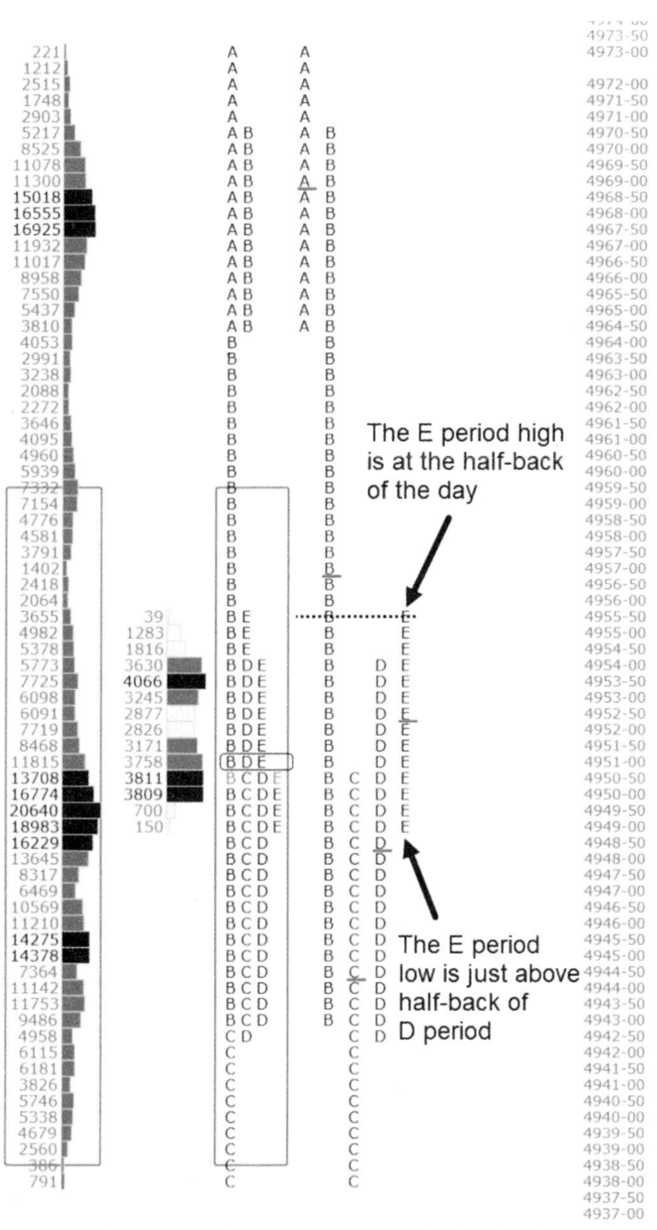

be relevant today or tomorrow, while being able to retrieve them when prices once again head that way. If you're not able to segregate nearby references from longer-term references, confusion is liable to rule the day.

It's easy to agree with this logic. But it's also easy to forget about it in the heat of market mayhem.

CHAPTER EIGHTEEN

THIS TIME IS DIFFERENT

You may have already guessed what's coming. Peruse the Profile in Figure 18.1.

On Friday, February 2, 2024, the market advanced sharply, following strong (and surprising) earnings from Meta. The ES tested the 5,000 level before backing off.

Over the weekend, I posted the following "Week Ahead" video on our YouTube channel (https://youtu.be/KAo0sR4QdXY): "This week's video will be in two parts. The first is direct and to the point for Monday morning's opening. The second part is more complex, exploring the relationship between momentum and market-generated information."

Part 1: "The last trade on Friday, as reported by the CME, was at 4,972.75, which is just slightly above Friday's center. The closer Monday opens to the center of the range, the greater the odds that we'll experience

Figure 18.1 The Profile Showing an Early Liquidating Break

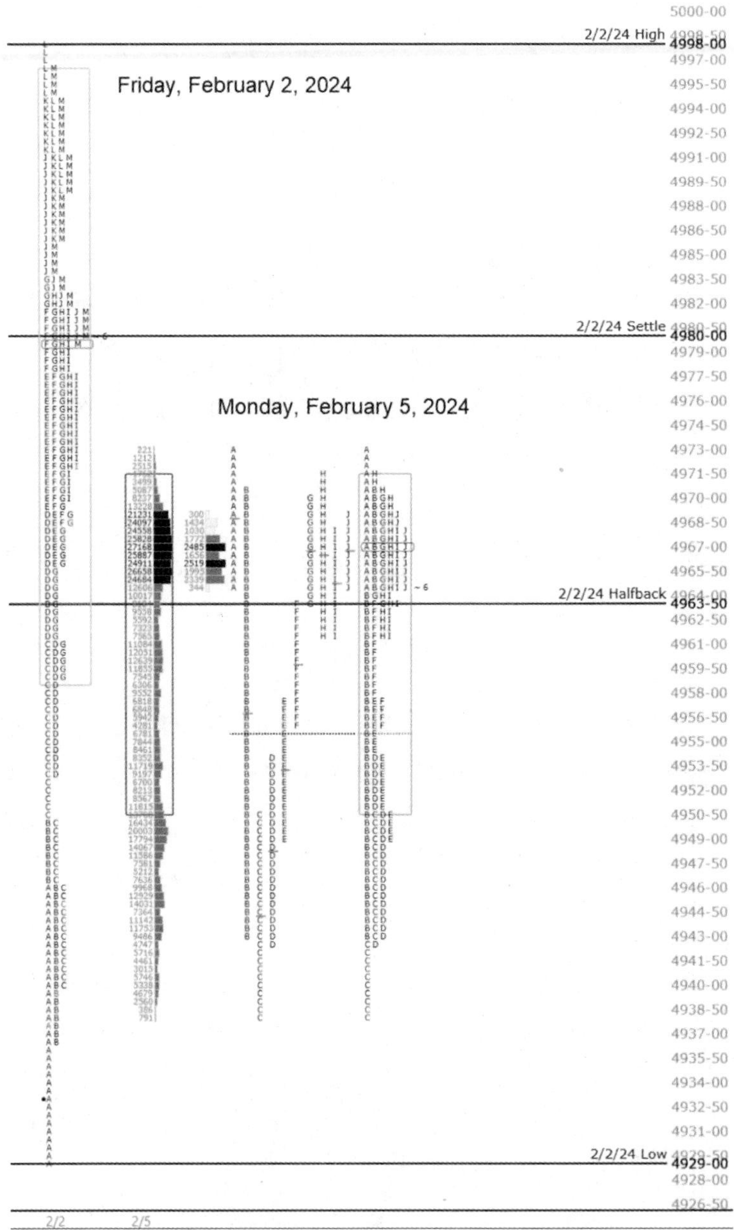

a rotational, balancing day. Opening well above the center of the range increases the odds that we will test Friday's high. Opening well below the center of the range increases the odds that we will test Friday's low."

Part 2: "Momentum is the market's leading indicator, with market-generated information (MGI) being the lagging indicator. Momentum is the leading indicator because of its simplicity to execute. MGI is far more complex, incorporating volume and market structure."

Then I defined the following potential scenarios:

- Momentum and MGI in sync – market is healthy with good odds of continuation.
- Momentum and MGI showing mild divergence – odds favor momentum continuation.
- Momentum and MGI showing significant divergence – counter-auction activity high.
- Friday's market showed significant divergence relative to both shape and volume.
- The shape, from the low to the high, was overly elongated, suggesting high emotional activity. Our emotional decisions aren't always reliable.
- Volume as measured via the NYSE was weak, particularly relative to the range. The commitment of buyers was low.
- I lean to the downside.

Monday morning, February 5, 2024, fixed-income markets gapped sharply lower (see Figure 18.2).

Additionally, on Sunday's *60 Minutes*, Fed Chairman Jerome Powell indicated the Federal Open Market Committee was wary of cutting rates too soon, and a rate cut in March was off the table.

Recently, the market had been responding negatively to rising yields, and there's an inverse relationship between bond price and yield. I was

Figure 18.2 The Gap in the Fixed-Income Market, February 5, 2024

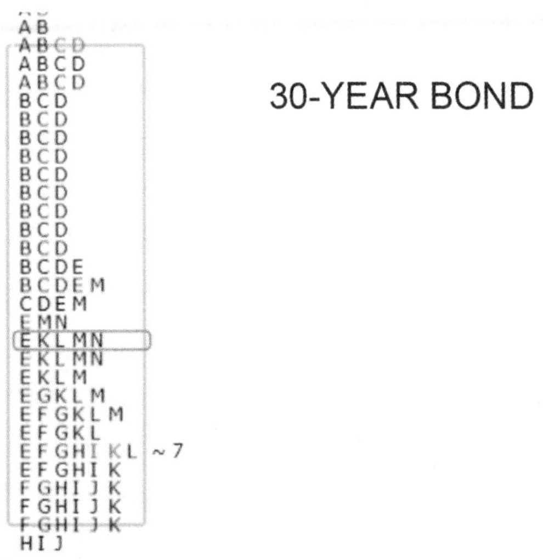

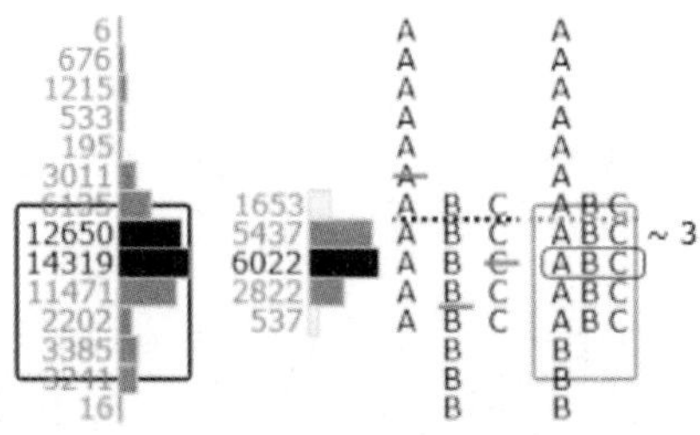

2/2 2/5

blinded by outside forces. Never take anything for granted or automatically assume a reaction to outside events.

The fact that there was not a continuing negative reaction to the rising yields pointed toward short-term strength in equities.

MONDAY'S MARKET ACTION

The following example *feels* simple to me as I relive it. When I read about something – as opposed to experiencing it in real time – I'm less emotionally involved, which makes it difficult to grasp the underlying importance.

To help you understand my thinking and emotional reactions, I'm presenting two versions. The first is an abridged, sterilized version. The second will be the unvarnished version, intended to convey a deeper understanding of the competing emotions in play.

Abridged

Bonds immediately gap lower. I recall the market's recent reactions – lower equity prices. Historically, I preach to trade the market based on its action, not what some other market is doing.

I've mentally prepared myself for lower equity prices.

Early conviction was neutral, which was confusing. However, my mind was fixated on the short side.

A delayed break in the ES confirmed my thinking.

The failure to take out Friday's low – suggesting that Monday was an inside, balancing day – was recognized. But I wanted to see lower prices and downward range extension to cover my loss from Friday, supporting my (unexamined) downward bias.

I recognized that tempo had slowed, which should have been a call to action to cover my short ES position, but my emotions refused to accept this market-generated information. I didn't listen to MGI, but MGI was correct.

This information is of no value if you refuse to recognize it.

Unabridged

The opening Monday morning was within a few ticks of the halfway point, relative to Friday's range. Consistent with the first part of the weekend's YouTube recording, the market delivered an inside day with the settle approximately at the center of Friday's range. MGI receives an A.

As measured by the Dow Jones, the early morning market was off more than 400 points, closing approximately 250 points lower. MGI again receives an A.

Your knowledgeable author, initially up a grand, ended the session with a $700 loss.

You can guess why: I struggled emotionally. I grappled with the decision to share what was occurring in the market, as well as what was going on in my head. All too often we hear what traders *say*, which isn't necessarily what they *did*.

Fear of missing out (FOMO) and my ego were the emotional factors driving my trading decisions. The ego came into play, as I was carrying a loss from Friday. The FOMO component relates to prior experience: Leading up to the 1973–1974 break, during the time of the "Nifty 50," there were similar underlying structural weaknesses.

The 1987 break, which was the biggest on record, also showed substantial underlying weaknesses. Had I taken my profit, I might have missed the biggest downside reference, which was easily within striking distance.

As a short-term day trader, none of the above is relevant. Similar thinking has undone many others. As a day-timeframe trader, the only thing relevant is *what other traders are doing*.

WHAT MGI TOLD ME ABOUT OTHER TRADERS THAT MORNING

I have continually stressed that early-morning confidence is one of the most important keys to short-term trading. Morning confidence on the 5th was extremely low. The market grudgingly tried to move higher, followed by an attempt to go lower, followed by another attempt to go higher, until it finally broke. Overall confidence was low.

The market opened approximately centered within the previous trading day's range; the odds favored rotation. We got rotation.

Examining the Profile in Figure 18.1, you'll observe what appears to be a liquidating break in the A, B, and C periods. Here's why I identified it thus:

- Confidence was low from the opening. If this were real, aggressive, *meaningful* selling, the odds would be better if the selling commenced from the opening.
- The market attempted to rally a couple times early in the morning. This increased the odds that short-term inventory was becoming long.
- The break did not take price outside of the previous day's range. Had the selling been stronger, Friday's low was easily within reach.
- Inspection of the Profile reveals an elongated structure, which is typical of liquidating breaks.
- Finally, tempo ground to a halt. In other words, the "offers" had dried up. Tempo often initiates the call to action. Which, in this case, would have been to cover my short.

As you have likely surmised, this is not a one-off occurrence. However, it has occurred less and less frequently over the years. The best tool I have to mitigate these circumstances is forcing myself to sit down and write out what happened – to articulate my thoughts.

I don't keep a trade journal that records each trade. Rather, I keep a *psychological* journal. Almost all of my issues are psychological or emotional, rather than related to market understanding.

I sincerely hope that this discussion will reassure you that you're not alone.

STAYING FOCUSED ON THE WAY TO THE FORUM

The following section wasn't part of the original book outline. But – markets seldom conform to my preconceived ideas, either.

"A Funny Thing Happened on the Way to the Forum" is a musical by Stephen Sondheim that chronicles the antics of a crafty slave who attempts to win his freedom by helping his young master. Thc plot is filled with mistaken identities, slapstick, and farcical situations as they navigate the bustling streets of Rome. Along the way, we witness a series of comedic misunderstandings and mishaps.

Sounds a lot like day trading.

As we recap the Profile in Figure 18.3 for the E-mini NASDAQ 100 for February 6, 2024, ask yourself if you would've gotten trapped by price. Sellers emerged early and consistently sold every rally until the last 90 minutes of the day. Staying calm and focused, in hindsight, is quite different than maintaining composure through five hours of constant selling on every rally attempt.

Figure 18.3 The Profile for the E-Mini NASDAQ 100 for February 6, 2024

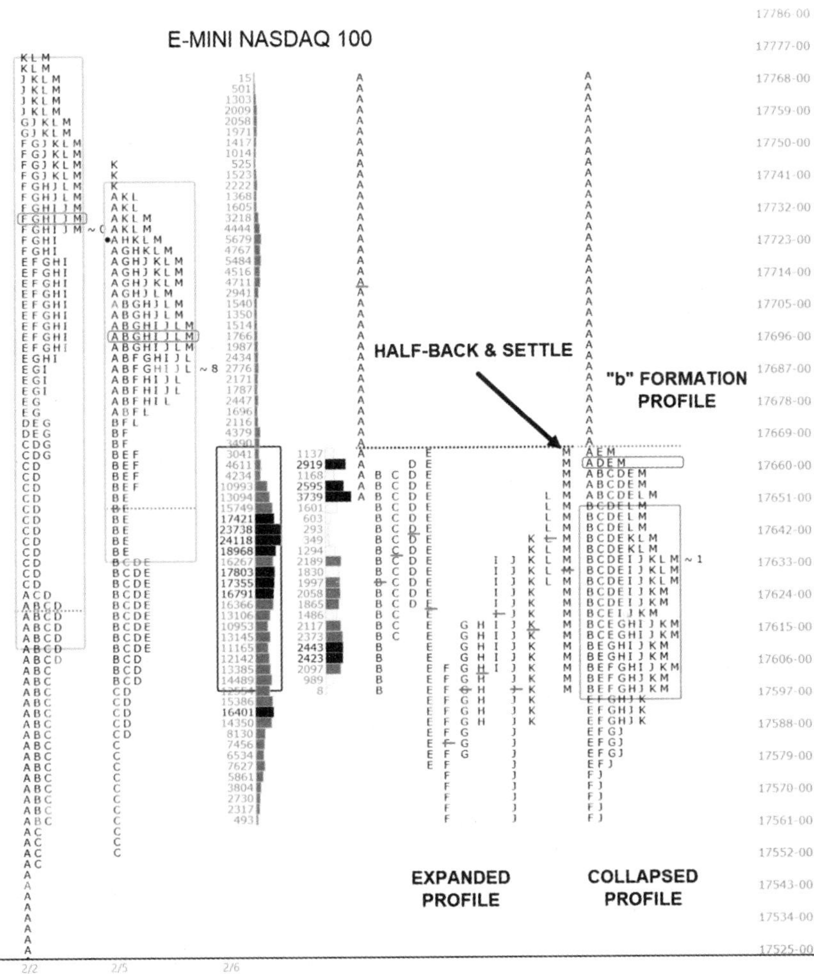

CHUNKING TOWARD SUCCESS

If you let yourself get focused on price alone, you're likely to miss the most significant information. This downhill spiral, for most traders, begins with price addiction.

If I query a trader about what occurred in the market on a specific day, they're likely to give me a linear recap. Conversely, the same query to an established, successful trader will likely include what *didn't* happen. In fact, repeating what we've said before, "What *didn't* happen is often equal to or more important than what *did* happen."

At this point, if you're scratching your head and wondering why this section header refers to "chunking," it's time for a reset. The constant selling during the first 10 periods – with rallies in-between – never traded to or below the previous session's low on February 5.

Chunking eases your mind away from price as you begin to envision the tell-tale "**b**" formation – liquidation versus new money. Prior to the market open, a quick review of the daily bars will remind you of the current trend, and chunking is activated.

HOW WELL DO YOU KNOW YOURSELF?

February 6 clearly provided meaningful short-term trading opportunities, both long and short. I have known few traders who can maintain a clear perspective while trading both sides of the market. We have written about self-awareness – this is an important subsection.

If it's a trending market, consider trading with the trend, which is far more forgiving if you're wrong. If it's a trading range or bracketed market, once you've identified the range, focus on your current trade location within the bracket. Solid trade location is a powerful risk-management tool.

One of the most challenging aspects of bracket or range-bound trading is the recognition that the best trades often fly in the face of the most recent market activity.

Before the market opened on February 7, 2024, E-mini NASDAQ Globex trade would open approximately 100 handles higher. The rally communicated significant electronic buying prior to the opening.

Throughout this day you could've easily gotten trapped by the continual selling. A more advanced view would have observed the selling relative to the market's inability to fill the gap. Short-term traders were getting short, and long-term traders were buying what they were selling.

SHORT IN THE HOLE

A frequent question asked during our intensives and public webinars is, "*How do you know when the market is getting too short?*"

Once a market has gotten too short, the slang is: "The market is short in the hole." This simply means that traders are short at bad prices.

The Profile in Figure 18.3 allows you to observe a market that's getting *short in the hole*. When inventory becomes too short, it can temporarily strengthen the market, as the shorts must eventually buy to cover their positions.

It's far too easy to get mesmerized by falling prices – without realizing the upside potential. Refer again to the earlier paragraph showing that electronic trade in E-mini NASDAQ was approximately 100 handles higher prior to the opening on February 7 (Figure 18.4).

Figure 18.4 The Profile for the E-Mini NASDAQ 100 Prior to the Opening on February 7, 2024

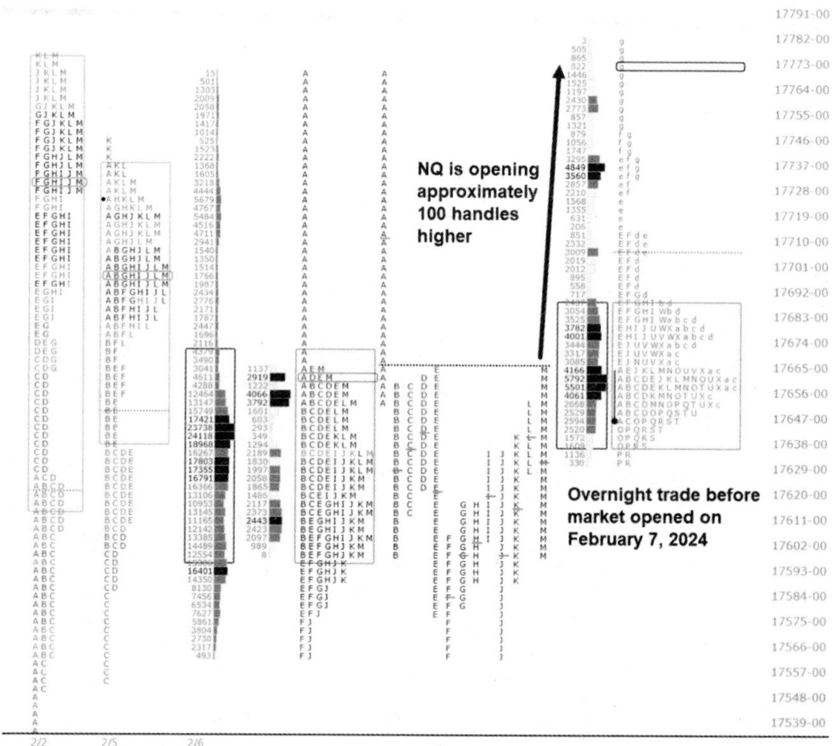

I'll leave you with this final thought: *Sometimes the best short-term opportunities fly in the face of the most recent market activity.*

Intuition is our most valuable compass in this world. It is the bridge between the unconscious and the conscious mind.

—**Josh Waitzkin,** *The Art of Learning*

CHAPTER NINETEEN

EMOTIONAL INTELLIGENCE: NAVIGATING SELF AND MARKET

While it's important to provide a foundational understanding of my market perspectives, the aim isn't to present a sanitized, step-by-step guide to financial gain through trading.

Trading doesn't accommodate false hopes; it demands a realistic approach.

February 13, 2024, laid bare nearly every emotion experienced by traders. To fully grasp this phenomenon, a background investigation is necessary.

Emotions were exposed as the Dow Jones Industrial Average experienced its most significant drop since March 2023, losing more than 500 points, or 2%, after being down more than 700 points earlier in the session. The S&P 500 and the NASDAQ composite followed suit, declining 1.37% and 1.8%, respectively. The catalyst for this downturn was the release of inflation data that surpassed expectations, diminishing the likelihood of multiple rate cuts by the Federal Reserve in 2024.

Historically, traders' *expectations* regarding the Fed's actions and its actual decisions haven't consistently aligned. As we say so often, hope is not a reliable trading strategy.

For the four months prior, the market had been one-timeframing higher. "Monthly one-timeframing" means that for each advancing month, the low from the previous month was not surpassed.

On Friday, February 9, for the first time ever, the S&P traded above and found acceptance beyond 5,000 cash (Figure 19.1). Upon close examination of this day's Profile, you'll see a double distribution (when there are single prints between distributions). As we covered earlier, each distribution is regarded as a separate day or auction.

Reviewing the Profile for Monday, February 12 in Figure 19.1 reveals that price traded below the single prints separating the distributions. However, there was no price *acceptance* within the lower distribution from February 9 – only single prints were observed at the low on February 12.

On February 12 two nuances caught my attention, both of which are significant for traders. First, the precision of the low stood out, nearly mirroring the low of the upper distribution from February 9. Such precision often suggests the involvement of shorter-term, weaker-handed traders. Second, the absence of excess at the February 12 high was notable.

Excess is a critical concept in our analysis, as it typically signals the conclusion of one market auction and the start of another. The lack of excess can often imply that short-term inventory has become overly long,

Figure 19.1 The Profile Showing a Double Distribution

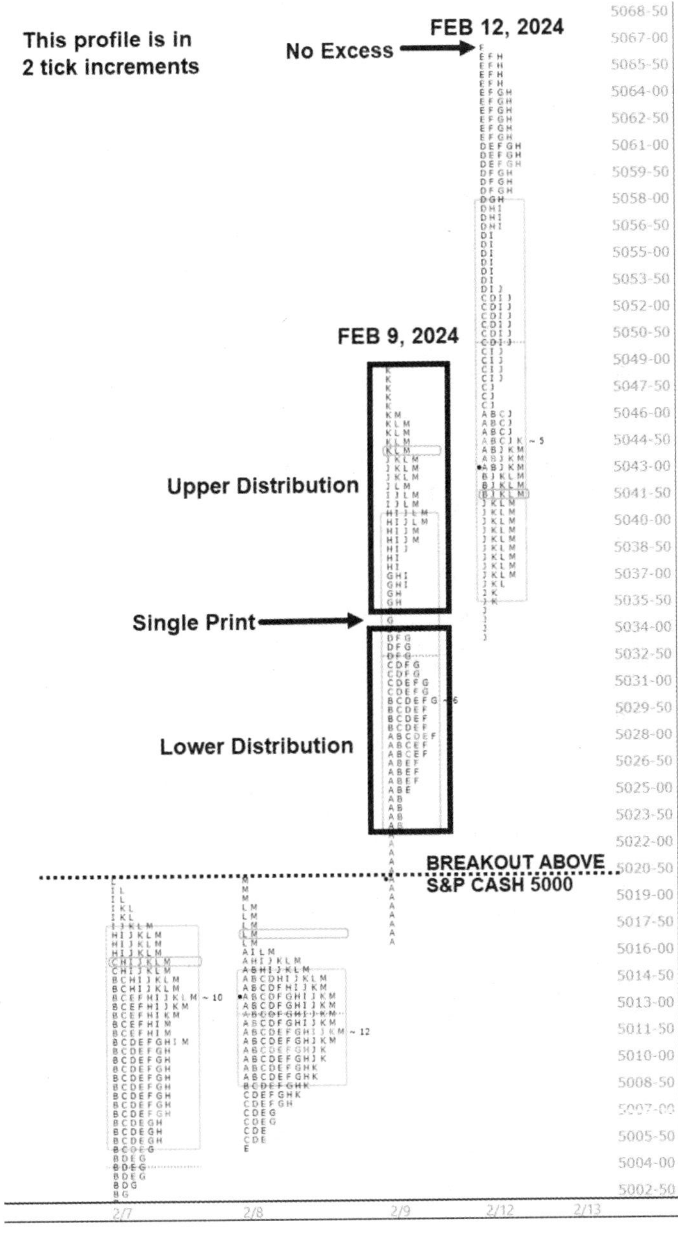

conveying a nuanced message about market dynamics. This can mean that inventory has temporarily become too long, restricting the market from advancing until inventory is rebalanced. Once inventory is adjusted, the market can continue its advance.

It's rare that a last auction is complete without excess. Mind the old trader adage: *Sometimes a market has to break before it can rally further.*

Earlier, we discussed the catalyst triggering the liquidation on February 13. The rationale behind this catalyst lies in a common trader behavior: Stick to strategies that have proven successful until they no longer yield results. In the lead-up to the market downturn, FOMO was driving the market higher.

THE WISDOM OF CROWDS

Prior to the close on Monday, February 12, ahead of the expected Consumer Price Index (CPI) report on Tuesday morning, the market sold off, closing near the low. I have seen this occur on many occasions.

In 1906, Francis Galton – a famous statistician and polymath – conducted an experiment entitled "Wisdom of the Crowd." A jar containing 800 beans was displayed at a county fair, and participants were asked to guess the number of beans in the jar. More than 100,000 guesses were collected.

No individual guess came close to the actual number; the closest was off by 80 beans. However, when the *average of all the guesses* was calculated, it was within two beans of the correct answer!

The market is complex. Attributing a single explanation for market action is extremely speculative. My observations, over the years, support observing *collective intelligence* when attempting to determine what might happen next.

TUESDAY'S GAP LOWER

On the surface, gap-trading guidelines are fairly clear cut: on a downward gap, sell when an early rally occurs, characterized by slowing volume and tempo. Tuesday's scenario deviated from these guidelines; it took more than three hours for sellers to overtake Tuesday's buyers (Figure 19.2).

Figure 19.2 The Profile of Tuesday, February 13, 2024

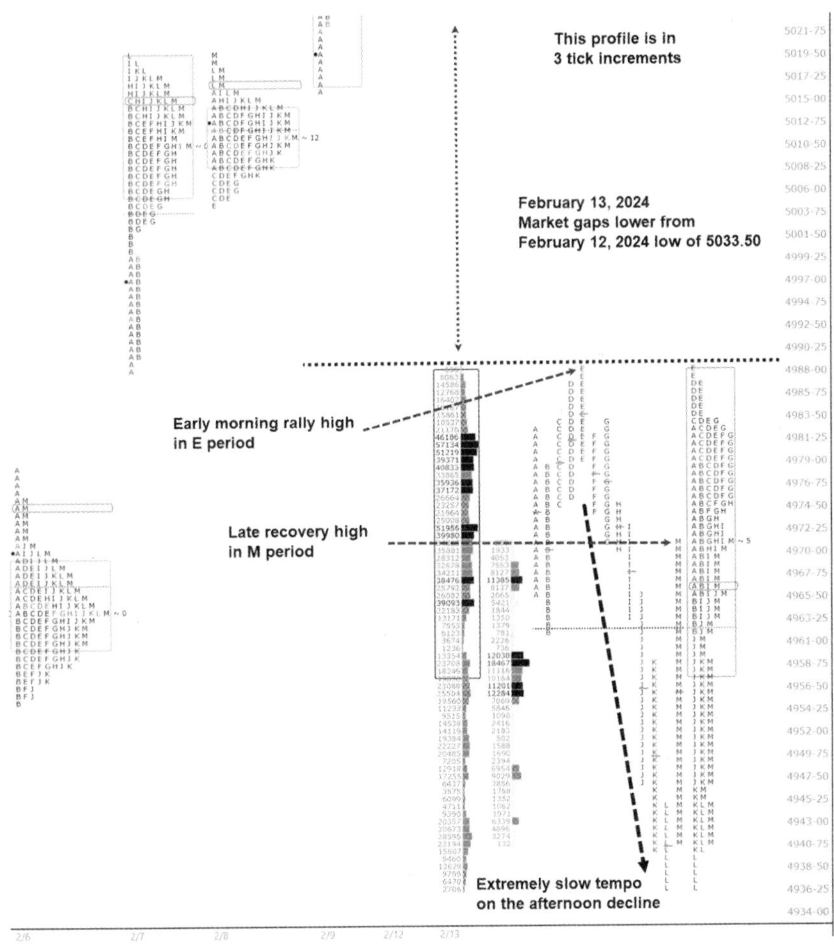

MARKET CONFIDENCE

For short-term traders, observing early market confidence – or lack thereof – can assist in mentally positioning yourself for the day. When confidence is high (within reason), there's a greater likelihood of seeing continuation relative to early confidence levels. Conversely, when confidence is low, there's a higher chance that the market will exhibit later rotation.

WHY DID THE MARKET DEVIATE?

There is never any certainty in the market. However, I speculated that early selling confidence was low, as neither investment money nor larger trading capital was interested in selling. If they were interested, it's unlikely they would've waited more than three hours.

Shorter-term traders were likely liquidating into the early rally. Once the liquidation began, the traditional follow-the-leader mentality took over, eventually leading to the market becoming too short.

Next, we'll discuss the assessment of how the market was communicating the fact that inventory was getting too short.

TEMPO

"Tempo" is defined as the speed or pace at which something progresses. It's not something that can be taught directly. Rather, it must be acquired through experience.

No matter how many NBA games you've watched, admiring the accuracy of three-point specialists, your ability to make that basketball shot yourself (in the heat of a game) is close to zero without the proper form, expertise, and endless repetitions. Similarly, mastery of a subtle concept like "tempo" only comes after accumulating significant skill and experience.

The tempo of price action on the afternoon of Tuesday, February 13, as the market traded sharply lower, was remarkably sluggish. While it's challenging to fully grasp this experience without witnessing it live, a thorough review of the Market Profile on this day will reveal the extent of the price drop, and the subsequent late recovery.

Learning to understand tempo doesn't come from books. However, the aim here is to emphasize the significance of tempo awareness. Internalizing the concept is a crucial step in setting yourself apart from your competitors.

EMOTIONS ASSOCIATED WITH TEMPO

The previous section offers a detached view of tempo, but once you internalize it, tempo can trigger a variety of actions (and emotions). Earlier in the book we referred to tempo as a potential "call to action." Let's explore potential actions from Tuesday afternoon, February 13, 2024:

1. Every trade has two sides – the entry and exit.
2. Tempo may prompt you to adjust a hedge.

This is a sterilized approach to tempo. Now let me recount the emotions I experienced that Tuesday afternoon. They were intense.

As I often invoke during webinars and seminars, "The best trades often defy the most recent market auction." Executing on this advice is challenging.

The decision to buy on Tuesday afternoon, February 13, was technically correct and well communicated via a slow tempo – but it felt nearly impossible. Watching the market plummet 700 points on the Dow, there were only two indicators suggesting a possible buy: The unusually slow tempo, indicating the market was likely overly short; and the market being only a few ticks above the January 31 high.

It's difficult to adequately convey the intense emotional turmoil that short-term trading can induce. Mentally preparing ahead of time is one recommended step; for instance, marking the January high on my Profile served as a useful reference point.

Observe your emotions as you trade and begin to develop an understanding of how your ability to reason can be severely hampered by unexamined feelings.

Life is a comedy to those who think, a tragedy to those who feel.

—**Jean Racine,** *Seventeenth-century French Playwright*

CHAPTER TWENTY

MARKETS IN TRANSITION

"Markets in transition" is an important concept, referring to extended periods of market consolidation followed by either trend continuation or reversal; markets seldom demonstrate a "V" or inverted "V" shape. When these "V" shapes do occur, they're often associated with unexpected black-swan events, and tend to be short-term and quickly corrected. Mistaking these unexpected auctions for changes in longer-term sentiment can be financially devastating.

For the discussion to follow, consider that markets usually progress from trend to balance (trading range), and then revert to the dominant trend or reverse direction. The difficulty in communicating this concept lies in the lack of a universal definition for "trend" or "balance." This is similar to people viewing a mountain range from different perspectives – from afar, they appear much different than when you're standing at the base. In other words, what you perceive relates to your distance (timeframe).

Shifting market sentiment is a *process*, not an instantaneous event. This distinction is important, as many traders judge too quickly, not considering that sentiment evolves gradually. This highlights the need for patience: *Avoid impulsive decisions based on short-term fluctuations.*

A complex interplay of myriad factors influences market sentiment. Recognizing that various economic, political, and psychological factors come into play helps avoid attributing changes in sentiment to isolated events – it's always more complicated than that. It's not uncommon for market conditions to suggest that change may be present; however, it sometimes requires a catalyst to actually *trigger* the change.

This kind of big picture mental preparation is vital for short-term traders.

BEWARE OF PROFESSIONAL TRADER BIAS

Professional traders' predictions regarding Federal Open Market Committee (FOMC) actions are historically inconsistent – sometimes surprisingly so – underlining the need for independent analysis. Avoid blind obedience to expert opinions.

Developing the ability to wait for the right opportunities while controlling emotional reactions to market movements is the hallmark of successful traders. Recognize that changes in sentiment are gradual, influenced by factors like inertia and confirmation bias. This ability (like all advanced abilities) can only be gained through active experience.

Monthly and weekly bar charts can help you distinguish between consolidating markets associated with trends, as opposed to markets in transition, which are usually more extended events. Incorrect assumptions can trap us into seeking only information that confirms our initial reactions, when in reality, different forces are at work.

In the heat of the moment, it's easy to lose sight of the fact that markets in transition often lead to a change in direction, but they can also resolve in a continuation of the original direction. Too many traders fail to consider the possibility of *continuation* when attempting to understand what kind of transition is taking place.

A discussion related to the graphic in Figure 20.1 will allow us to better visualize multiple occasions followed by transition or continuation. (Remember, trading is an art, and not everyone will agree with the way I label the elements in Figure 20.1.)

Figure 20.1 A Broader Perspective of the Markets via Monthly Bar Chart

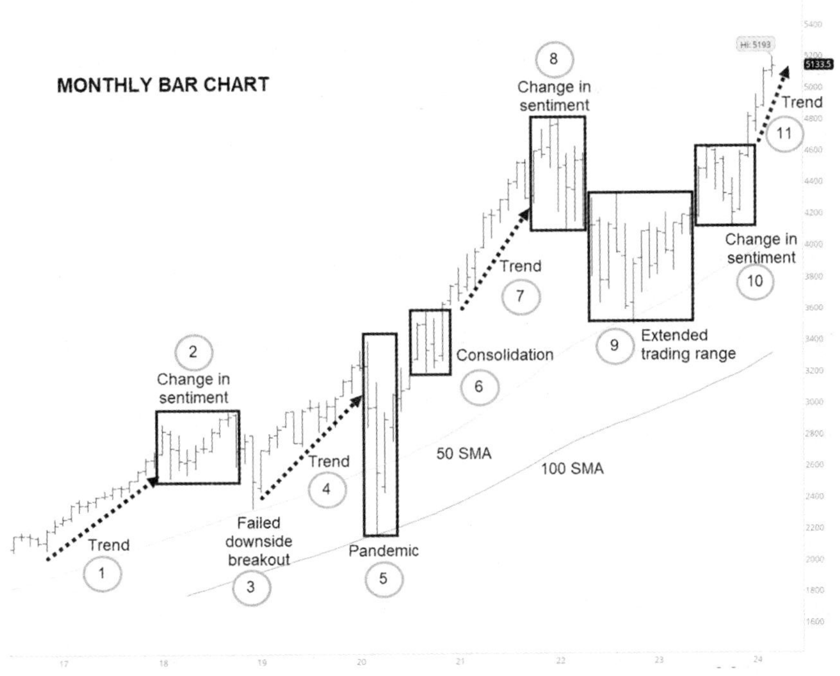

As a short-term trader, my perspective often gets overly focused on the short term by the end of a trading session. To overcome this bias, the first thing I do after the market closes is review the longest timeframe by assessing the monthly bar chart, seeking to gain a broader perspective. Only then do I refine my focus through the weekly bar.

Let's review my market observations from the monthly bar in Figure 20.1.

1. *A multi-month trend is underway. No matter what biases you have, trading with the trend is the optimal strategy. This means buying breaks and taking profits on rallies.*

   Many traders can't help themselves and rush to short higher prices in these kinds of circumstances. It's not uncommon for traders to begin their careers favoring reversion-to-the-mean strategies.

   Don't stick your head in the sand. A daily trade-tracking log can help prevent reactionary tendencies, as it provides a larger context for understanding what's really happening. As someone who has been severely challenged by these kinds of market movements over the years, I can't emphasize this enough: *Don't fight trends.*

   If you can't resist and find yourself shorting an upward trend, you want to be right almost immediately. During these periods I constantly review the weekly and daily bars, along with Profiles, to better refine entries and exits. Many traders will lose track of the larger trend, which negates opportunity.
2. *The market has transitioned from trend to trading range.*

   The monthly bar continues to suggest that the long-term trend remains higher. Without reviewing the monthly bar each day, it's extremely difficult to maintain this perspective. Weekly and daily bars – along with daily Profiles – help you narrow your short-term perspective.

For the last five months in this trading range, the market had one-timeframed higher. This is consistent with the long-term trend.

3. *It is unusual to see a gap occur on the monthly bar (monthly gaps are rare and Figure 20.1 does not have a gap in the monthly bar). Monthly gaps indicate a rapid change in sentiment, often related to some kind of black-swan event. As we wrote earlier, these events are often followed by relatively quick recoveries.*

   Reading about this is unlikely to supercharge your emotions. However, being actively engaged in the market during these periods can be very challenging emotionally. When volatility increases rapidly, there is no shame in stepping away for a few days until the market clarifies itself. The danger of remaining in these markets is twofold: first, a loss of financial capital, but more importantly, the risk of losing substantial *emotional* capital.

   I believe that emotional capital is the more important of the two.

   The downside breakout fails at the 50-month moving average. While I'm not a technician, I do plot the 50-day, 100-day, and 200-day moving averages on the daily bar chart, as they are widely followed by multiple timeframes. I pay close attention to the 200-day moving average, as it garners investment attention.

4. *The market returns to trend for the next 13 months. Numbers 1, 4, 7, and 11 in Figure 20.1 all represent upside trends. As traders, we are overwhelmed with short-term stimuli that can feed our biases – either positively or negatively. The daily review of the monthly bar chart will help you remain focused. Again, the first thing I do following the market close is review the monthly bar for perspective.*

   Trading against the trend is the fastest way to lose your capital. The most positive approach to trading is buying strength – unless the trend shows weaker volume on rallies and higher volume of pullbacks, stay with the trend.

5. *The pandemic was a black-swan event and was short-lived. The U.S. stepped in with both fiscal and monetary policy changes to stem the decline.*

   The downside breakout fails at the 100-month moving average.
6. *The application of fiscal and monetary policy stemmed the break related to the pandemic, returning the market to prior levels. Uncertainty was high, and the market remained in a tight balance for the next four months.*
7. *A classic breakout from the four-month balance, with the market trending higher for the next 13 months. Viewing the upside breakout after the fact – when your emotions are not involved – is straightforward. Following pandemic volatility and a four-month balance that puts you to sleep, it can be hard to believe the breakout is real.*

   Daily preparation, starting with the monthly bar, creates the best odds for getting onboard the trend. Once the trend is underway, seek to continually maintain perspective: Start each day by reviewing the monthly bar, which will strengthen your confidence to remain with the trend.

   Along the way, there will be experts who disagree with the trend. There will be an equal number of experts projecting even higher levels.

THE BIGGEST OBSTACLE TO STAYING WITH THE TREND IS YOU

The weekly and daily bars will occasionally expose you to counter-auctions, which are healthy relative to the longer-term trend, as they allow inventory to rebalance. This all seems very logical in the safe environment of reading a book. However, as a human, your instincts will most likely work against you – confirmation bias may be at work, as many experts will disagree with the rally.

8. *To understand Number 8 in Figure 20.1, start by looking at the last monthly bar in Number 7. Now look at the first monthly bar in Number 8. Notice the distance traveled from the low in Number 7 to the high in Number 8. I grew up north of Chicago in a hilly section surrounding a lake. My red wagon always ran fastest at the bottom of the hill.*

   You are observing the laggard buyers.

   The fourth bar in Number 8 shows a non-linear break in the market; notice how this follows the laggard buyers. Without a deeper understanding and appreciation of how the market works, you're likely to be confused and get whip-sawed. Watching laggards top a market is confusing as prices often move rapidly.

   Doing your (often tedious) daily preparation – starting with the monthly, weekly, and daily bars – provides you with the best odds of keeping your perspective sharp and your emotions in check. I have learned the expensive way that you're often better off being a little late rather than a little early when markets transition.

   The final three months under Number 8 demonstrate balance, and balance-trading guidelines are applicable to all timeframes.

- If you're a very short-term trader, an inside 30-minute bar would represent balance.
- A slightly longer timeframe trader might consider two or three overlapping 30-minute bars as balance.
- Progressing toward longer timeframes next might be an inside day followed by two overlapping days, etc.
- Our current discussion, under Number 8, views the final three months as balanced.

Balance-trading rules are as follows, to refresh your perspective:

- Remaining within balance further tightens the balance.
- Go with any breakout from balance. This will be dictated by your timeframe.
- Fade or go against any breakout that fails. On a failed breakout, the potential destination is the opposite end of the balance area.

9. *Following the downside breakout from the balance seen in Number 8 above (Figure 20.1), the market entered a 12-month trading range.*

Notice the failed upside breakout in the fourth month. Reflect again on the balance-trading guidelines.

10. *This six-month trading range was extremely difficult, as the market never clearly distanced itself from the previous trading range. The monthly bar is only the starting point to maintain perspective. The weekly and daily bars allow you to more cleanly hone your shorter-term trading perspective.*

11. *The breakout from the six-month balance shown in Number 10 (Figure 20.1) saw the market transition back to trend.*

Chapter 21 gets granular about the importance of preparation, repetition, and the path to a balanced approach to trading.

I never won a fight in the ring. I always won in preparation.

—Mohammed Ali

CHAPTER TWENTY-ONE

EXPLICIT/ IMPLICIT LEARNING

As you have undoubtedly noticed, we're now delving deeply into real-world market examples to provide context and color to the fundamental concepts described in the first half of the book. As we progress through these illustrations, I will occasionally evoke the difference between *explicit* and *implicit* learning.

Explicit learning involves the conscious acquisition of knowledge and skill through direct instruction and deliberate practice. You are aware of what you're learning and can articulate what you know. Implicit learning, on the other hand, occurs unconsciously through exposure to information and experience. This form of learning leads to the acquisition of knowledge and skill *without conscious awareness* – you can't necessarily articulate what you've learned, but you're still influenced by it. Implicit learning comes from repeated practice and experience.

Let's return to our baseball analogy to make this real. Hitting a baseball involves a combination of explicit learning – which involves conscious instruction, analysis, and decision-making strategies – and implicit learning, honed through extensive practice and experience. Both forms contribute to a player's ability to succeed at the plate.

Explicit learning involved in hitting:

- **Instruction and feedback:** Coaches provide precise instruction on hitting techniques and strategies, offering feedback on mechanics, approach, and decision-making.
- **Cognitive strategies:** Players employ cognitive strategies like visualization to enhance focus and performance.
- **Pitch analysis:** Coaches and players analyze pitch data, studying video footage to identify patterns and weaknesses in opposing pitchers.
- **Plate discipline:** Players learn to recognize pitches outside the strike zone through conscious decision-making.
- **Adjustments and problem-solving:** When faced with challenges or slumps, players seek explicit advice from coaches and make deliberate swing adjustments.

Implicit learning involved in hitting:

- **Motor skills acquisition:** By repeatedly swinging the bat, players develop muscle memory (chunking) for proper mechanics, such as stance, grip, and swing path.
- **Perceptual abilities:** Players subconsciously learn to judge the speed, trajectory, and spin of an incoming pitch, allowing them to anticipate where and when to swing the bat.
- **Timing and coordination:** Over time, players learn to sync their body movements with the pitch's arrival without needing to consciously think about it.

- **Adaptation to variability:** Implicit learning enables players to adapt to the variety of pitch types, adjusting their swing based on subtle cues in the pitcher's delivery and the ball's flight path.
- **Pattern recognition:** Players develop an intuitive sense of pitch patterns and tendencies, enabling them to anticipate pitch types and locations based on situational cues.

TAKE ME OUT TO THE MARKET

Applied to trading, it's easy to see (from this distance) that both explicit and implicit learning inform your ability to step up to the plate and execute a trade. Less experienced traders usually rely more on an explicit approach to trading, mechanically applying the rules they've learned. More experienced traders, on the other hand, tend to rely more on their intuition born of experience – the deeper, less obvious results of implicit learning.

As you read at the outset of this book, *trading is a nuanced art.* That means developing a balanced approach that incorporates the nuts and bolts of explicit learning with the nuance of all those "at bats," when your subconscious steadily built a foundation of understanding that cannot be easily quantified in a "here's how you trade" book.

Thus the long list of trading methods and philosophies that, followed explicitly, don't tend to result in profits. Many hedge funds and commodity trading advisors – having failed to develop an *implicit* understanding of the nuances of trading – have introduced *explicit* programs that result in sharp ups and downs. (I don't have statistical evidence of this, but I doubt that there is much consistency in this approach.)

In my online and real-time trading courses, oriented toward day and short-term trading, one of the most common questions I'm asked is, "*Do you offer setups?*" The answer is a resounding (if disappointing) "No!" If setups were actually available, they would be arbitraged away immediately by large, computer-based trading firms.

We have turned away many potential clients when we recognized that they're simply not mentally or emotionally ready to begin the extremely difficult task of becoming a profitable trader.

Now let's examine explicit and implicit learning in the context of trading.

EXPLICIT LEARNING INVOLVED IN TRADING

Trading methods are acquired through textbooks, courses, webinars, and other structured learning processes. Learning how to use market-generated information includes the construction of the Market Profile, value areas, point of control, gaps, etc. – all explicit indicators.

Larger concepts can be explicit as well, such as learning to identify trending markets versus balancing markets, and how the market transitions from one to the other. You learn the mechanics of strategies associated with breakouts from balanced markets, for example, along with frameworks for developing your own style and approach.

It's important to acknowledge that explicit learning often leads to a false sense of confidence, along with a rigidity that blocks your ability to integrate implicit knowledge, only developed after many, many at-bats (so to speak).

Overdependence on explicit learning can virtually guarantee a negative outcome. Take note of warning-sign questions you may ask yourself without considering the larger context of momentum and timeframe: *Where do I enter? Where do I place a stop? When do I get out?*

The constant need for exacting answers can alert you to this overdependence.

Trading without taking the time to develop implicit learning is dangerous. Without a sound foundation earned from countless hours of observing market behavior, you're like a loose leaf buffeted by strong winds.

IMPLICIT LEARNING INVOLVED IN TRADING

Through repeated exposure to the intricacies and endless varieties of market behavior, you begin to recognize patterns associated with long liquidation and short covering, for example. You develop your intuition, like a batter who starts to get a feel for the nuance of how a curve ball leaves the pitcher's hand.

Intuition complements your explicit knowledge, and you begin to sense situations that can lead to short covering and long liquidation before they become manifest in the tell-tale "**p**" and "**b**" formations.

Through implicit learning and reflection, you develop emotional intelligence that gives you the opportunity to make rational decisions, unaffected by surges in heart rate when fear, envy, or desire limit your brain's abilities and cause tunnel vision.

Implicit learning increases your flexibility to adjust to constantly evolving markets. And you only get it by stepping into that batter's box, again and again and again.

EXPLICIT–IMPLICIT INTERACTION

Your foundation of market understanding is developed by gathering explicit knowledge. Then, over time, implicit knowledge begins to help you refine and adapt that explicit knowledge to the endlessly interactive world of trading.

The two forms of learning are complementary and must be balanced. Over-reliance on explicit learning leaves you too inflexible to deal with rapidly changing markets. Without a solid foundation, the odds of getting whipsawed greatly increase.

Repetition with variation, combined with focused mentorship, helps refine your intuition and emotional control. Tracking your trades can provide valuable insights into the way your emotions affect your execution and overall market approach.

Markets are dynamic – what works today may be a terrible strategy tomorrow. Explicit knowledge is too slow and inflexible to adjust to changing market conditions, while implicit knowledge is faster and more intuitive.

Explicit learning precedes implicit learning. Explicit learning is constant and deliberate, while implicit learning is unconscious and automatic. The final goal is to develop a *feel* for the market that lets you pick up subtle clues from price movements, news events, and other market data. You'll be able to adapt your trading approach based on past experiences and intuition, avoiding common trading mistakes without constantly analyzing them.

Balance the explicit and implicit and you will improve your ability to react quickly and instinctively to market changes; you'll be well on your way to becoming an expert trader.

> I think about baseball when I wake up in the morning. I think about it all day and I dream about it at night. The only time I don't think about it is when I'm playing it.
>
> —**Carl Yastrzemski,** *18-Time All-Star, Member of the 3,000-Hit Club*

CHAPTER TWENTY-TWO

EVOLVING INTUITION

Most traders overlook the pivotal role of intuition in achieving trading success. Among the recommended readings integral to this book is *Gut Feelings: The Intelligence of the Unconscious* by Gerd Gigerenzer. More on Gigerenzer in a moment, but first let's revisit the notion that momentum trading is the primary approach employed by short-term traders – despite its often poor results. When you integrate market-generated information (MGI) into momentum trading, you add crucial *context* to the decision-making process. Great thinkers all the way back to the Greek philosopher Heraclitus emphasized the importance of *context* in learning.

MGI + context: This concept can pave the way for the evolution of your intuition.

YOUR ONGOING LEARNING JOURNEY

For more than 40 years, I've endeavored to empower traders with market-generated insights. Unfortunately, many traders only seek such information after they've faced many failures. They often underestimate the complexity of trading as a pursuit, so that when they finally turn to MGI, they're already inundated with misinformation.

As we often state: *Unlearning is a significant challenge.*

Trading cannot simply be "taught"; it must be *self*-taught. Two essential components of this process involve self-awareness and your subconscious. The journey begins by acknowledging the potency of intuition, then actively working to enhance it.

Intuition undergoes a fascinating transformation as it evolves, shaped by experience, expertise, and context. Gerd Gigerenzer's exploration in *Gut Feelings* underscores a central theme: **Less becomes more as intuition matures.**

Consider the journey of a novice, for whom simplicity and deliberate focus are paramount. I always advise novices to concentrate and take their time, accumulating explicit knowledge to enhance their performance and refine their instincts.

As one progresses along the path of expertise, the landscape shifts; what once propelled growth may now inhibit it. The seasoned professional requires a different approach that embraces complexity and allows for fluidity of thought. In this evolution, the intuitive process transcends mere concentration; it becomes a nuanced interplay of knowledge, pattern recognition, and swift decision-making, where the subtleties of intuition dance harmoniously with the complexities of experience.

Gigerenzer's insights illuminate not just the development of intuition, but also its adaptive nature, reminding us that in the realm of intuition, the journey from simplicity to complexity is a dynamic voyage. It might seem paradoxical that as you gain experience and market knowledge, the principle of "less is more" becomes a vital component of nuanced trading.

> I believe that all wisdom consists in caring immensely for a few right things, and not caring a straw about the rest.
>
> **—John Buchan**

An example from Gigerenzer will help you internalize this discussion. A novice and an experienced golfer were each told to take their time, check their stance, etc. before hitting the ball. The novice performed better than normal, while the experienced golfer underperformed.

In this traditional "speed-accuracy trade-off," thinking too much about the process can actually disrupt performance.

THE POWER OF INTUITION

Markets can change quickly following breakouts, news announcements, and other events. In these moments, when time is limited and information is incomplete, our honed intuition can be invaluable for making rapid decisions in a chaotic environment.

Pattern recognition based on experience can empower us to draw conclusions without constantly having to analyze every possible detail. In fact, getting lost in details can cause us to overthink the situation, or respond too slowly to capture opportunity. In addition, conventional logic/analysis often inhibits the creative process; we want to trust the experts, systems, and emotional whims that constantly besiege us as we watch markets unfold.

True intuition, on the other hand, is based on deep market understanding, and should not be considered a "knee-jerk reaction."

For the expert, emotional intelligence has been constantly refined through experience. By the time explicit clues have surfaced, short-term opportunity may have passed and less experienced traders are left flailing in the aftermath.

Many inexperienced traders fail to understand the extended process by which intuition becomes reliable, and so become overconfident in their nascent "intuitive judgments." The higher the stakes, the greater the consequences of this kind of overconfidence. Over the years, I've noticed that the people who tell me that they're "fast learners" tend to be the same individuals who make these kinds of destructive decisions, based on hunches rather than deep pattern recognition.

Our personal biases, emotions, and past experiences can weaken our intuitive ability. An honest self-assessment is critical in constantly reassessing our intuitive skill, and if necessary, setting a corrective course.

Intuition is often unreliable in unfamiliar situations. The influx of new money into the stock market following the COVID-19 pandemic is an example of a situation in which intuition became less reliable; substantial numbers of first-time traders, flush with COVID-19 funds, changed market complexity in perplexing ways.

Intuition is not a substitute for critical thinking and rational analysis. Recognizing the strengths and weaknesses of intuition is a powerful component of successful trading.

INTUITION OF THE MASTERS

I will end this chapter with a brief review of the way three brilliant minds describe intuition: Garry Kasparov, the highest rated chess player in the world for more than 20 years; Josh Waitzkin, a dual champion in chess and martial arts who was portrayed in *Searching for Bobby Fischer*; and Roger Martin, author of *The Opposable Mind.*

Kasparov acknowledges the importance of intuition in both chess and life. In his teaching, intuition refers to the ability of experienced players to make quick decisions based on patterns and a deep understanding of the game. Intuition allows a player to assess a position rapidly, choosing the most promising course of action without necessarily being able to articulate the precise reasons behind the decision. Kasparov emphasizes that intuition is not a substitute for calculated analysis, but rather a complement to it.

Waitzkin emphasizes the need to develop intuition through deep understanding and practice. He describes intuition arising from a combination of knowledge, experience, and pattern recognition. A deep intuitive understanding can only be gained by immersing yourself in the subject, repeatedly engaging with its complexities and nuances until you don't have to actively "think" about what to do next. The best players seamlessly integrate calculation and intuitive judgments, with intuition playing a central role when split-second decisions are required that don't allow for conscious deliberation.

Martin suggests that intuition is not purely innate, but can be cultivated and refined over time with experience and reflection. He encourages individuals to trust their intuition while also honing their critical thinking skills in order to ensure a balanced approach to decision-making. He believes that intuition is most valuable when faced with uncertainty or incomplete information.

These three masters agree that success is enhanced by the ability to harness both rational analysis and intuitive insight, empowering us to remain calm and focused in ambiguous situations, when incomplete information makes rapid decision-making uniquely challenging.

This philosophy is perfectly applicable to short-term trading.

CHAPTER TWENTY-THREE

BRINGING IT ALL TOGETHER

From this point forward, we'll focus on examining individual days and the nuances associated with trading these sessions. The following examples come from March 5 and 6, 2024. As a reminder, successful short-term trading is often highly dependent on what happened prior to the current trading day.

BACKGROUND

The market continues to trend higher with a series of new all-time highs. For the past five months, the market has been one-timeframing higher.

1. On the morning of March 5, 2024, the market gaps lower on news that APPL's sales in China have declined sharply. APPL and other tech stocks have been under pressure for some time.

2. Notice that the shape of the early Profile in Figure 23.1, from the high to Number 2 looks like the letter "**b**." Earlier we described this formation as representing a liquidating break. Learning to interpret this kind of structural clue is pivotal to translating market-generated information (MGI) into action.

   A liquidating break represents an imbalance in selling long positions – old business. While there will naturally be some new selling, the prominent business is liquidation of existing positions.

   We're often asked, "*How do you know the market has gotten too short?*" You can never be sure. However, learning to read and interpret structure and MGI puts you in a better position to make this judgment.

3. The movement from Number 2 to Number 3 is most likely the result of shorter-term traders misinterpreting the earlier price break. Most traders operate purely from the point of view of price, making no distinction between liquidation and new-money selling. Liquidation can in fact *strengthen* the market, as it removes overhead resistance. Remember, "*Sometimes markets have to break before they can rally.*" Weaker hands are replaced with stronger hands.

   Almost all market breaks begin with liquidation. If there is a healthy combination of liquidation and new-money selling, the structure of the Profile is likely to be more elongated. A solid combination of liquidation and new-money selling produces higher odds of downside continuation.

   Later in the session – K and L periods – short-term traders again begin to sell, forcing price lower. Traders were getting caught "short in the hole," or short at poor prices. Additionally, tempo was extremely slow on the afternoon of March 5, suggesting that laggard traders, following only price, continued to sell the market.

   Tempo can't be taught; it is only learned through experience. In addition, tempo can't be universally applied, because tempo with

Figure 23.1 The Profiles of March 5, 2024, and March 6, 2024

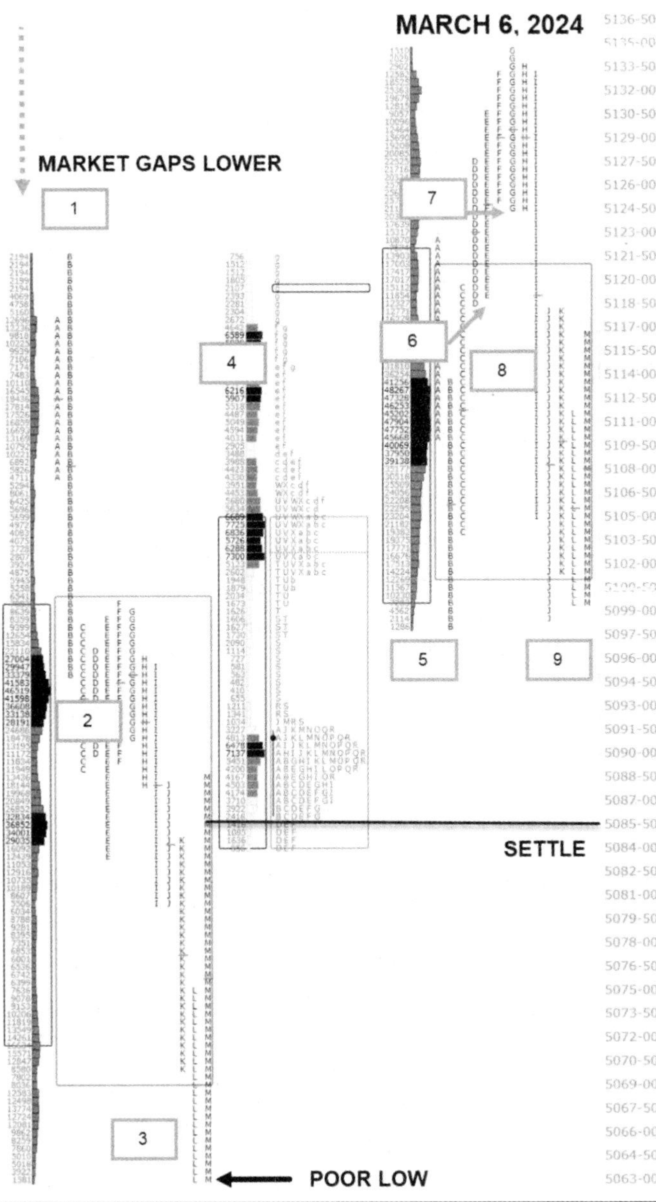

the trend is usually interpreted differently than tempo against the trend. Slowing tempo *with* the trend often means that directional activity is slowing down and may indicate that inventory is rebalancing. Slowing tempo *against* the trend often provides an opportunity for traders who are on board the trend to add to their positions, and for other traders to participate in the trend.

Review the "settle" in relationship to the low for the session and you'll see confirmation of the late short covering.

The center Profile records overnight trade. It's not unusual for overnight trade to continue in the direction last witnessed during New York Stock Exchange hours.

The observation revealed in Number 3 relates to the "non-excess" low. When traders are caught too short, it's not unusual to witness this kind of low. To better appreciate this nuance, reflect on how you feel once you realize that you're caught short – when the market trades near the low, there is a sigh of relief as you cover. Once the short covering gets underway, buying begins to feed on itself.

4. As a review, overnight inventory is measured from the settle to the overnight high or low. In the current example, the settle it is at 5,085.50 with the overnight high being at 5,121.50 – overnight inventory is long.

   Approximately 75% of the time, the ES (E-mini S&P 500) experiences a counter-auction relative to overnight inventory. If overnight inventory is long, the counter-auction would result in selling. The odds turned out to be reliable, as selling occurred following the opening.
5. The liquidation of overnight inventory drove the market down to the 5,100 level where buyers re-emerged (remember, the long-term trend is up). As a general rule, when the trend is up, the most productive strategy is to buy breaks, taking profits on rallies.

Buying the break at the 5,100 level would've been consistent with this strategy.

6. Once you're engaged in a trade (in this example, a long), your focus is on monitoring for completion. The two most complex, pivotal concepts we introduce in our educational programs are "Let the trade come to you" and "Monitor for continuation."

   Observation – the first step in chunking – reveals that the D and E lows were almost matching. This kind of nuance only gets noticed with time. The almost-matching low is characteristic of the action of weaker day-timeframe traders. In other words, the odds are that the buying at the D and E lows were not from longer-term traders or investors; shorter-term traders have limited staying power.

   Recognizing who you're competing against is one of the most important steps in becoming successful.

7. The almost matching F, G, and H lows (chunking continues) are communicating the compounding risk of holding long positions.
8. I and J periods represent the culmination of MGI observed under Number 6 and Number 7 above.
9. When prices decline, as they did under Number 8, traders immediately begin to speculate on the nature of the selling: was it primarily liquidation, or a more potent combination of liquidation and new-money selling?

The market's inability to meaningfully extend below the 5,100 level implies that we witnessed liquidation, rather than the more potent option. Exacting levels like 5,100 often convey multiple messages. The first is that short-term traders accept this level as "support." The second message, because of a lack of lower excess, suggests a dearth of interest from longer timeframes. This observation helps us understand that the odds suggest this level is temporary.

CHAPTER TWENTY-FOUR

MARKETS HANDLE CURRENT BUSINESS FIRST

Short-term trading, heavily orientated toward day trading, is extraordinarily challenging. As of this writing in late March 2024, short-term trading is attracting the largest volume and participation; options volume alone is reportedly similar to New York Stock Exchange (NYSE) volume.

Markets must deal with immediate activity before pursuing their larger purpose, which is to serve as a platform for buying and selling shares of publicly traded companies, providing liquidity for investors, and enabling corporations to raise capital. That immediate interruption often takes the form of a widespread emotional reaction to a news event, which can result in temporary inventory imbalances, followed by short-covering rallies or liquidation breaks as the markets seek to rebalance inventory.

Because this kind of reaction is common, an *exception* to the customary, emotional knee-jerk response can signal that significant change is underway. The most common exception occurs when the market is balanced in a tight, well-defined trading range. This sort of "balance area" indicates the market is waiting for new information before beginning its next directional auction.

Reviewing March 18–20 as a continuum highlights some of the challenges faced by short-term and day traders. A review of the chart in Figure 24.1 shows the long-term trend is clearly up, with the monthly bar one-timeframing higher for the previous five months.

Figure 24.1 Long-Term Trend in the Monthly Bar Chart

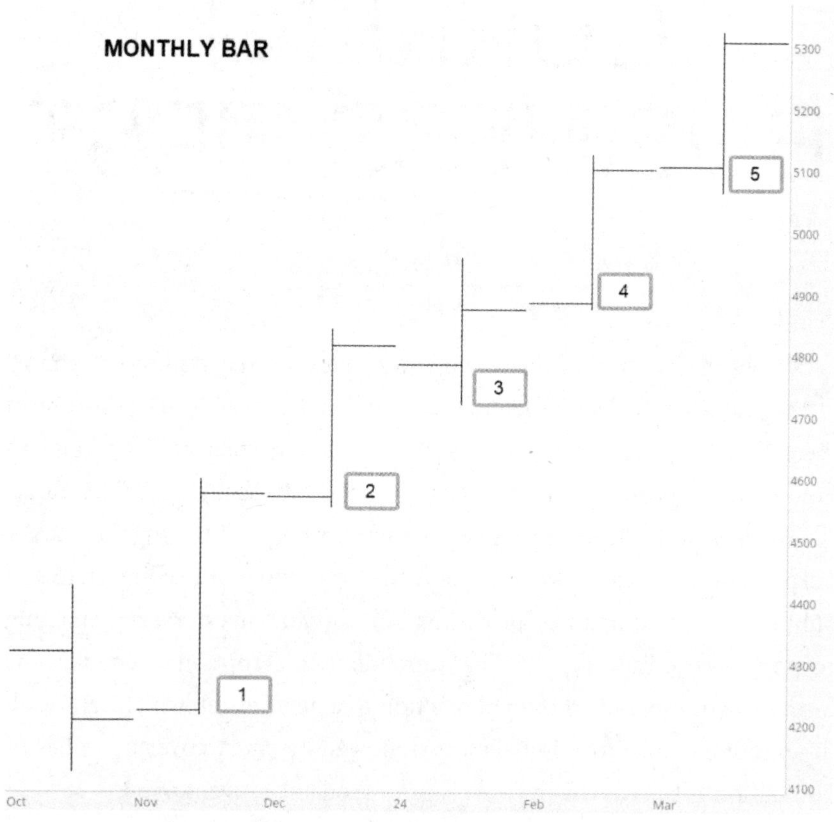

A closer inspection, via the daily bar chart in Figure 24.2, allows us to observe the low-confidence environment preceding March 18, 2024 – for the prior 17 trading sessions, there was no continuity or direction.

Figure 24.2 The Daily Bar Chart, February 5–March 20, 2024

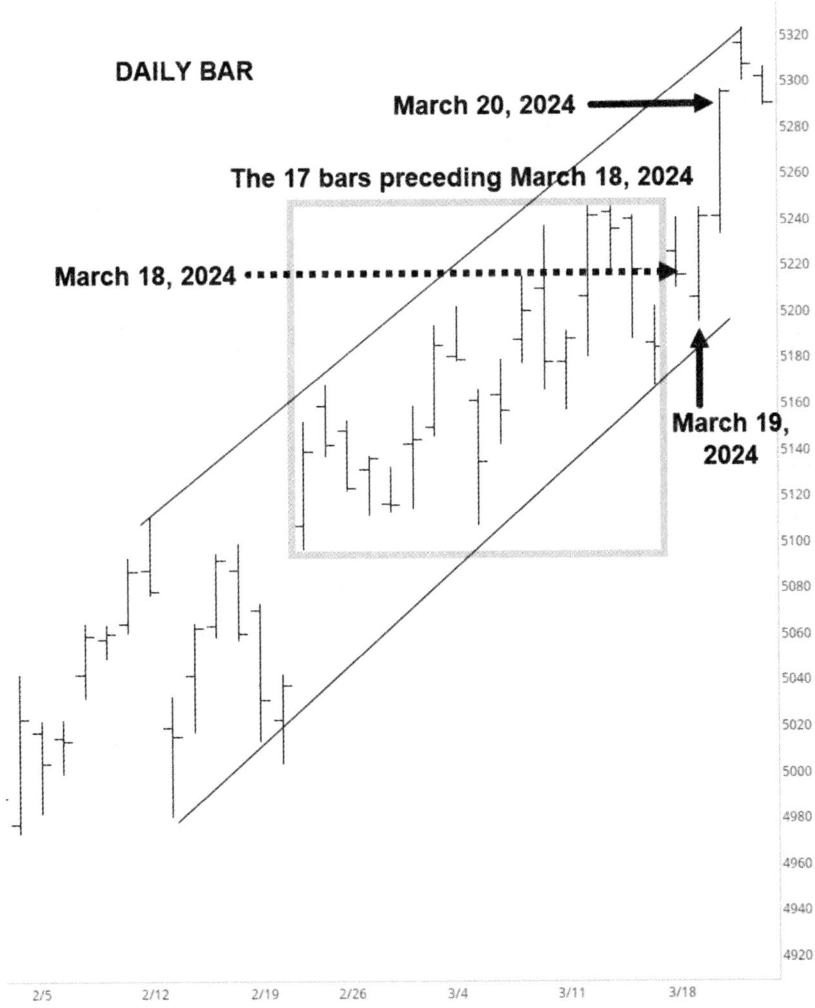

Figure 24.3 The Profile Showing Gap Higher on March 18, 2024

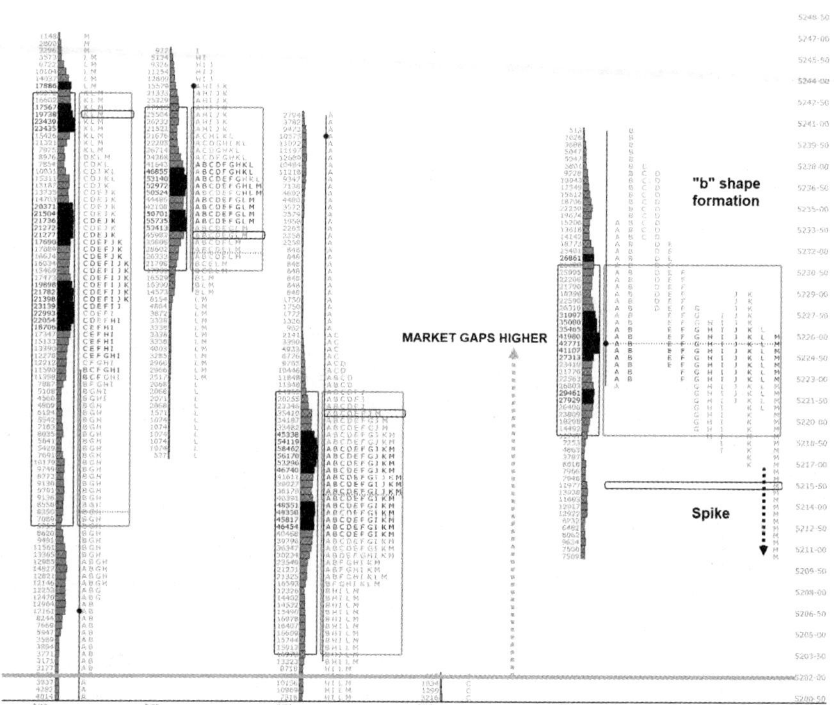

On the morning of March 18, positive news led the market to gap higher on the opening (Figure 24.3). (Refresher: Gaps, either up or down, are measured from the previous day's high or low – not from the settle.)

The biggest challenge for short-term traders is to react to current business.

The biggest challenge for slightly longer-term traders is to recognize what's happening in the shorter term, without losing perspective of the larger context.

In this three-day example, the cross-currents between day-timeframe and longer-term information are extremely challenging. (I've often

Figure 24.4 The Daily Bar Chart for February–March 2024

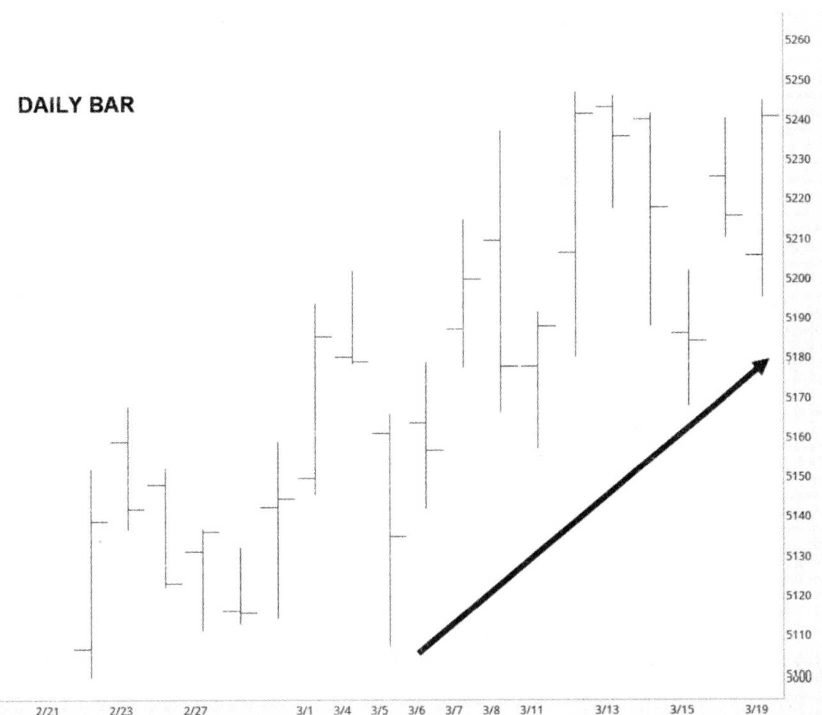

confessed to reading certain books and passages many times before finally appreciating the depth and complexity of the author's message.) Beyond-day-timeframe traders may be better equipped to take the 18th in their stride if they're clearly focused on the longer trend – which is not to imply they should overlook this trading session! By fully appreciating what happened on March 18, they are better equipped for what occurs on the following days.

Let's unpack this concept by examining the challenges of dealing with "current business." #1–#8 refer to Figure 24.3; #9–#15 refer to Figure 24.5; #16–#19 refer to the daily bar chart in Figure 24.4.

Figure 24.5 The Profile for March 19, 2024

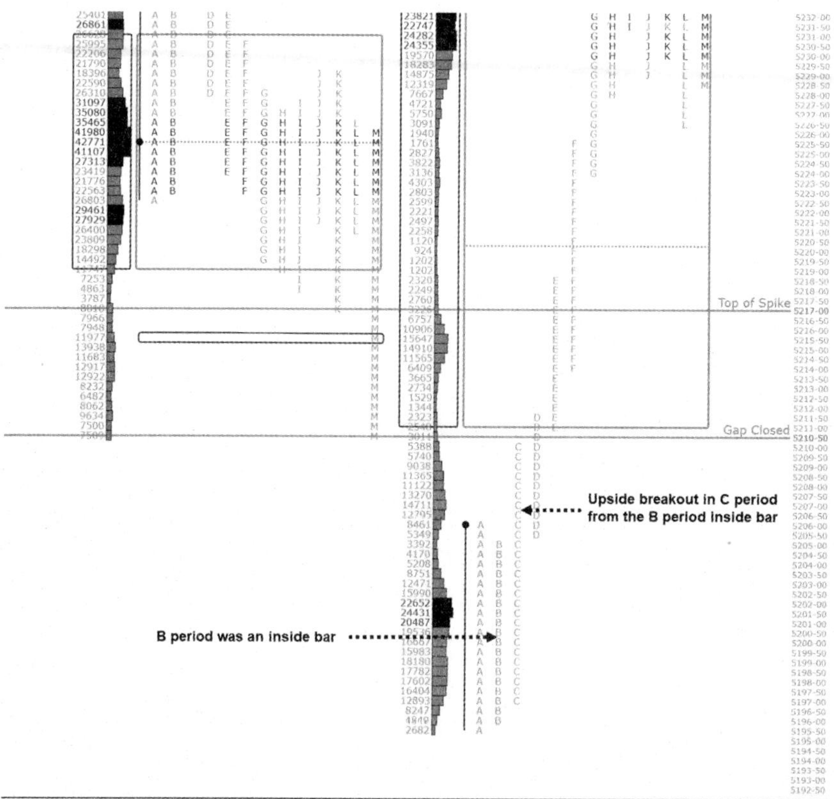

1. The market gaps higher with A and B periods lows almost matching. While the gap holds, the proximity of the two lows suggests relatively low confidence.

   Day-timeframe traders are advised to go with gaps, then monitor for continuation.
2. B period rallies to within a few ticks of the high on the 14th. This is an important day-timeframe high for the day trader.
3. The longer-term trader should notice the accumulation of highs from the 12th, 13th, 14th, and 18th. This higher level is finding more and more price acceptance.

4. C period delivers an inside-balancing bar.
5. The day trader, if they have not already exited a long, should exit as D period trades below the C period inside bar. Balance-trading guidelines are applicable to all timeframes.
6. The structural "**b**" formation of the Profile communicates liquidation, rather than a more potent combination of liquidation and new-money selling.
7. The structural message should be recognized by longer-term traders as positive for future upside continuation. Only the most experienced, attuned traders will recognize this combination of factors: the accumulation of highs from the 12th, 13th, 14th, and 18th; followed by the "**b**" formation; and liquidation on the 18th – these add up to support of upside continuation.

   Understanding the complexity of the 18th and its conflicting messages is where the "rubber meets the road," if you're to survive as a trader.
8. Reviewing the 18th, observe that the final M period presented traders with a downward price spike – exploration late in the day when there wasn't enough time to determine if the spike was accepted or rejected. Here are a few spike guidelines:
   - **(a)** The top of the spike in a downward spike is *resistance.*
   - **(b)** Trading within the spike during the following session represents acceptance of the spike.
   - **(c)** Trading above the top of the spike on following days communicates that prices had not only traded low enough to cut off selling, but had traded low enough to attract *buyers.*
9. The market gaps lower on the 19th. Here are a few gap guidelines:
   - **(a)** Go with gaps that aren't filled in fairly quickly.
   - **(b)** The best short opportunity on a downward gap occurs on an attempt to fill the gap, when both upward volume and tempo slow.

On a short, monitor for continuation. As prices trade lower, downward continuation should come with lower prices, lower value, and increasing volume.

Trade location helps maintain perspective. The following daily bar graphic in Figure 24.4 illustrates the importance of trade location on the morning of the 19th. There are a lot of moving pieces, each of which can challenge your objective perspective with conflicting emotions.

10. The market failed to carry higher on the 18th, with a lower price spike late in the session.

Overnight witnessed downward continuation followed by a lower gap opening, then downside follow-through early on the morning of the 19th. A quick review of the bar chart provides important information about trade location. Your daily preparation should have identified the long-term trend was up, or up and balancing.

The early downward price exploration on the morning of the 19th was originally inconclusive. Reference graphic in Figure 24.5.

11. The upside breakout from the B period inside bar was an alert that change was possible.

12. Notice that the C period high was a single tick from closing the gap – this important nuance indicates that sellers, from such an exacting reference point, are likely to be weaker, day-timeframe traders with limited staying power. As the market has broken to the upside from the early morning low and inside bar, the odds favor upside continuation.

13. Closing the gap increases the odds of upside continuation. This is more likely following the morning's downside test, followed by the upside breakout of the B period inside bar.

14. The top of the spike from the 18th is resistance. Trading above the spike continues the positive auction.
15. From the upside breakout in C period, the market one-timeframes higher for the next six 30-minute periods.
16. The final trading period again approaches the cluster of highs discussed earlier. This greatly increases the odds of upside continuation because excess is limited here, which indicates the cumulative acceptance of price at higher levels. The market has continued to balance, and the longer the balance, the greater the odds that a breakout from that balance will be dynamic.
17. Finally, you will recall that balance is the market's plea for additional information, prior to beginning a new auction. Markets progress from trend to balance, or from balance to trend.
18. On the 20th (Figure 24.2), the release of the Federal Open Market Committee's March statement was that "new information" the market was waiting for.
19. Balance trading guidelines are once again in play.

This sequence of days provided an excellent example of the many ways information can be confounding, if not viewed in the proper context. No matter what your trading timeframe is, you will benefit from balancing an understanding of the market's longer-term motivation with the immediacy of the day's unfolding indicators – which often conflict and confound, leaving novice traders grasping at anything that will confirm their preconceived notions.

It's a useful exercise to try and *feel* the emotions that might have raced through your nervous system on these days. As I've repeated a thousand times before (and will repeat until the end), *everything is a series of facts surrounded by other circumstances.*

During the sequence of days discussed in this chapter, it would have been easy to get lost focusing on the single factor of *price*, ignoring the influence of *time* and *value*. You must keep your mind in equilibrium, balancing your understanding of longer-term market momentum with the insights that emerge from MGI, as revealed in the unfolding structure of the Market Profile.

The biggest decision you make daily is what to focus on.

—Shane Parrish

CHAPTER TWENTY-FIVE

MAKING DECISIONS (IN THE HEAT OF THE MOMENT)

Short-term traders face a relentless barrage of incomplete information. Many fall prey to information overload, failing to discern what truly matters within the current context. Successful traders, on the other hand, are able to filter this barrage, focusing on the indicators that support meaningful action.

The late afternoon of March 26, 2024, serves as a solid illustration of this reality (Figure 25.1). On the 26th, within a framework that perceived the long-term trend was upward and balancing, value was developing higher.

Figure 25.1 The Profiles from March 20 to March 26, 2024

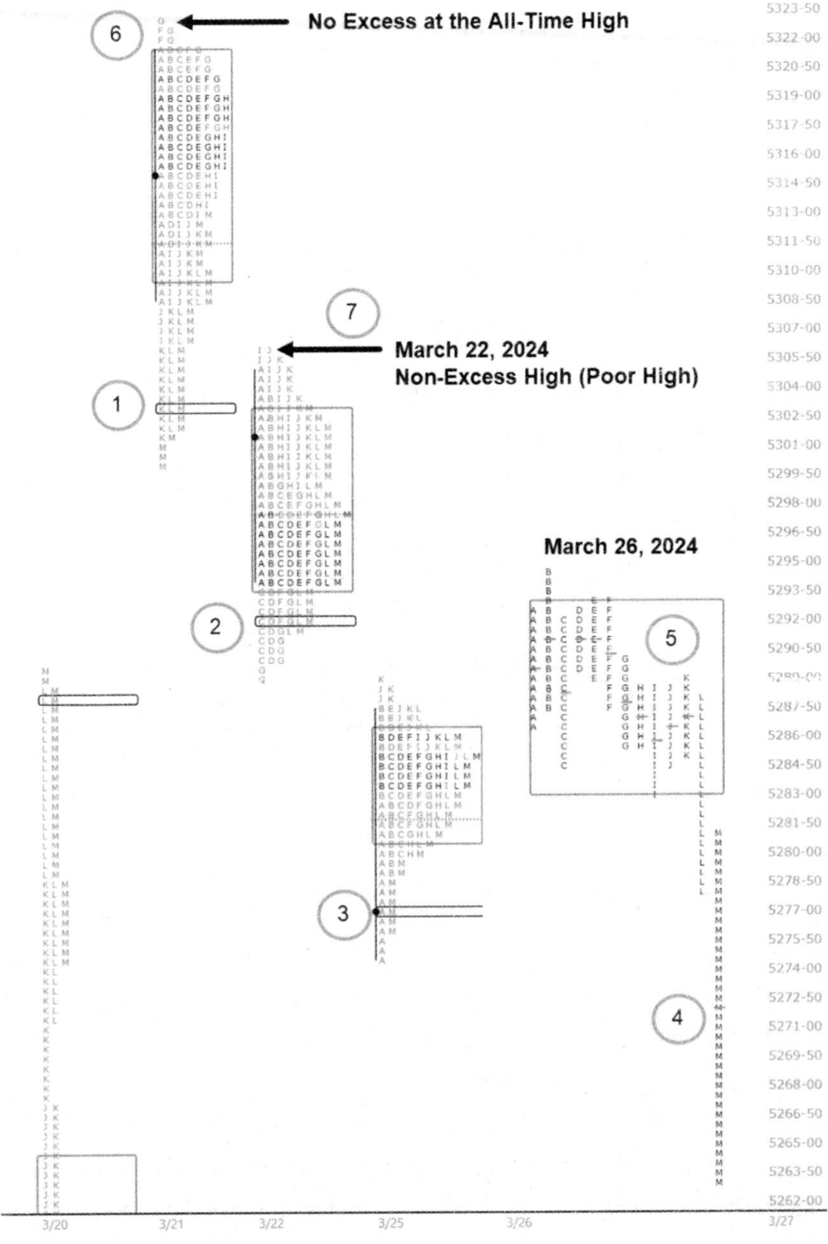

General guidelines advise trading with developing value, but following that theory blindly can lead to disappointment.

A broader observation reveals a recent pattern adopted by short-term traders (Figure 25.1):

1. On March 21, short-term traders liquidated late in the session.
2. The same liquidation pattern recurred on the 22nd.
3. Similarly, it was observed again on the 25th.
4. Without recognizing this pattern from preceding sessions, traders were likely to get caught off-guard when the market suddenly shifted late in the afternoon on the 26th.
5. Highs in periods H, I, J, K, and L were all comparable. Based on previous observations and experience, it was likely that these highs would be surpassed. A few reminders are pertinent here:
   (a) Trading is more art than science.
   (b) Probability does not retain memory.
   (c) Intuition may sometimes defy the odds.
6. The example in question is in two-tick increments, and there was no excess at the all-time high.
7. There was no excess on the 22nd. The absence of excess can sometimes indicate that short-term inventory has become excessively long.

I began this chapter on decision-making with this unusual example to underscore that while rote learning is a standard starting point, it alone will not set you apart from the competition; it's merely the first step on the long journey to becoming a proficient trader.

Too often, traders strive to compete by fixating on the same references as everyone else. While these references are relevant, achieving success in short-term trading demands unwavering focus, imagination, and creative problem-solving.

Successful trading is process-driven, but once your process is well-defined you must become adept at recognizing *anomalies* and *nuances*.

TRADERS DO WHAT WORKS – UNTIL IT DOESN'T

As I'm in the process of writing this book, I'm pleased that the market has once again provided a marvelous piece of serendipity with this challenging example. Consider this chapter a practice test: If you want to gain a glimmer of the challenges of short-term trading, thoroughly *own* this chapter before moving on, without putting any time constraints on yourself.

A recap of the previous example: Short-term traders pressed the sell side at the end of the day for three days in a row. By the fourth day, March 26, 2024, short-term traders sold en masse as the day was ending (Figure 25.1). The 26th strongly demonstrates thc action of short-term traders who frantically sold and sold and sold… until inventory was dangerously short. This is an exceptionally clear example of the process by which a market becomes short-in-the-hole (short at poor prices).

You can begin to understand why a market that becomes too short has also accumulated *short-term strength* – buying is required to rebalance inventory. Momentum traders are prone to attribute strength to the short covering, which can weaken a market as the conditions that drove buying no longer exist. In fact, it's not uncommon for momentum traders to take inventory from too short directly to too long.

Yes, this is complex! Which accounts for the high rate of failure.

It's unlikely that you'll be successful by simply focusing on references. Short-term trading is a game, and like any game, understanding your competition and how they act is required to be competitive.

By the time the market opened on the 27th, price had returned to the high of the 26th.

The following requires intense concentration: While prices rose overnight, the odds were that the market remained very short. Only a small percentage of day-timeframe traders trade overnight (we don't have data on this, only years of observation).

The graphic of the 27th is provided in Figure 25.2.

Figure 25.2 The Profile on March 27, 2024

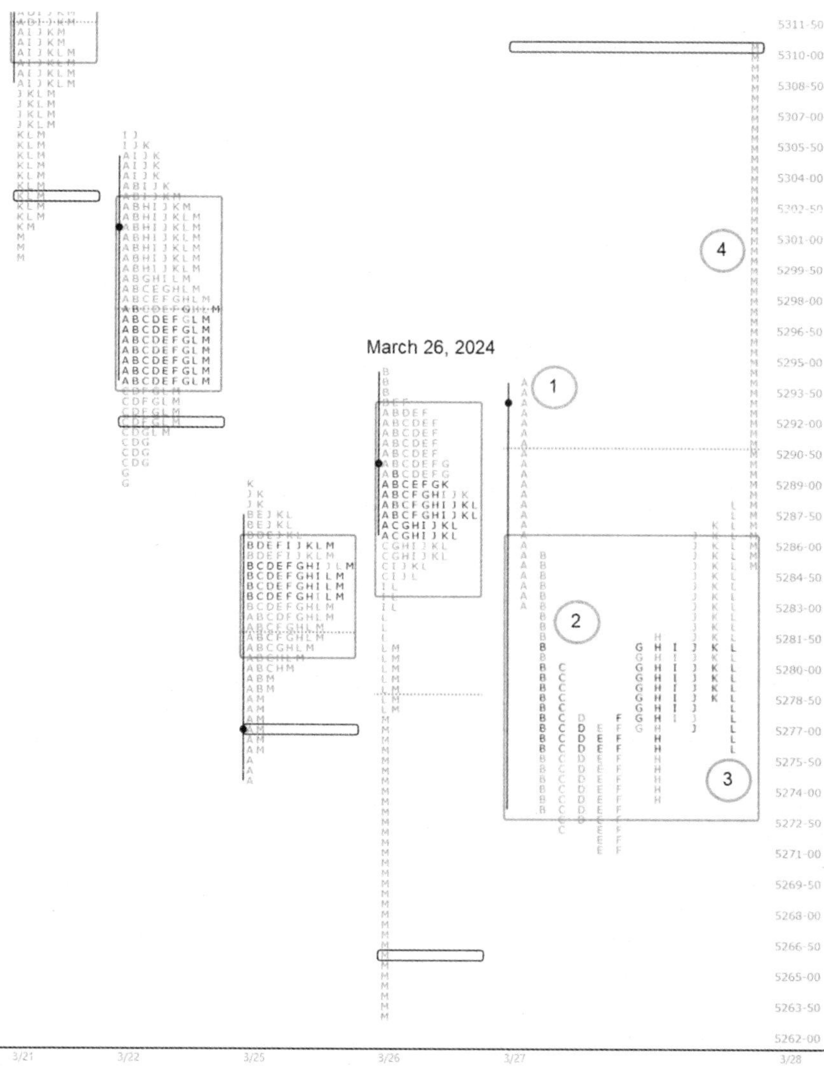

1. By the morning of the 27th, the market opened near the high of the 26th. When dissecting the 26th, we focused on the comparable H, I, J, K, and L highs. The odds were against these almost-matching highs lasting for an extended period. These extremely mechanical highs are often the result of very short-term, day-timeframe sellers. This type of high has high odds of being revisited, and the opening on the 27th supported this analysis.
2. Short-term traders, having seen the market decline the previous afternoon, sold into the opening. Because most short-term traders don't trade overnight, inventory is likely becoming even shorter as short-term traders were selling from the opening.
3. Late in the afternoon, traders – who had become conditioned by witnessing the market sell off late in the session for the last four sessions – begin to sell. The trap was set.
4. As short-term traders began to sell late on the afternoon of the 27th, the shorts from the previous session and before were caught short, and a massive short-covering rally was underway.

This is much simpler to write about than to execute.

On the afternoon of the 27th during K period, I suspected what was about to occur. As price initially traded lower, my emotional response was to short. However, experience told me the odds of a short-covering rally were high; the best way to participate was through the purchase of out-of-the-money calls.

We'll round out this chapter by continuing through Thursday March 28, which was also the end of the first quarter.

My goal has been to present the 26th, 27th and now the 28th as a continuum. You will know that you are fully engaged when you feel immersed within these three days (Figure 25.3).

Figure 25.3 The Profile on March 28, 2024

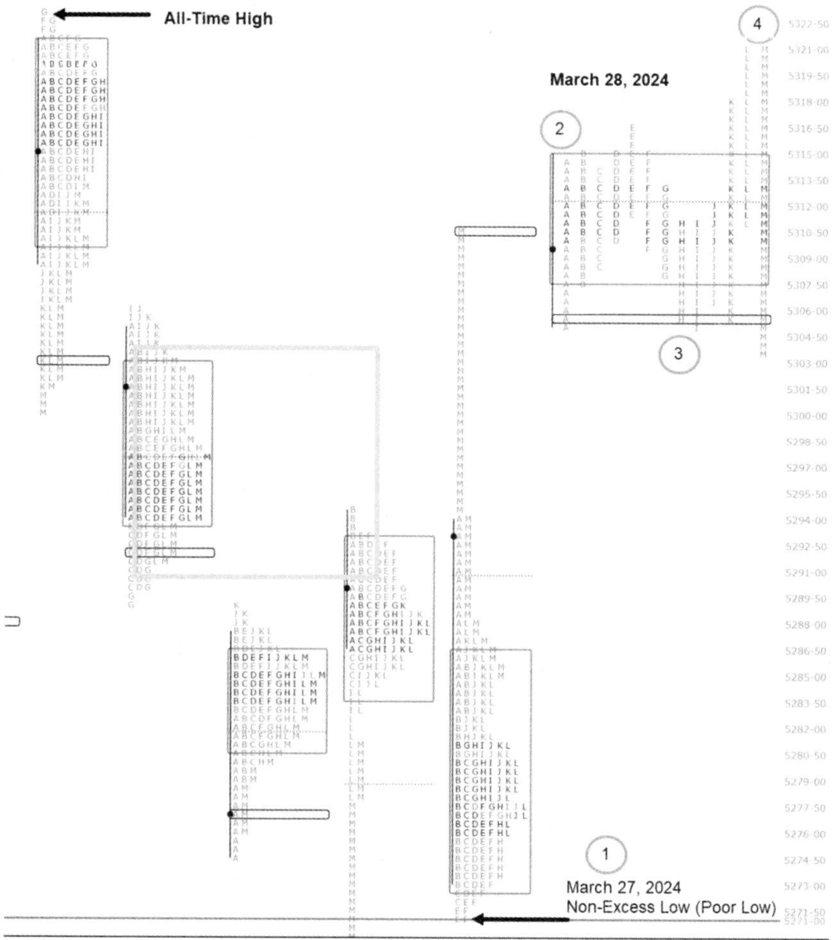

1. One data point you should be carrying forward, as trading opens on the 28th, is the non-excess low from the 27th. It's only a single data point, but you should be fully aware of it.
2. On the morning of the 28th, the market attempted to extend the short-covering rally from the 27th.

Notice the "**p**" shape of the early rally, which represents short covering rather than a more robust combination of short covering and new-money buying. The odds of upside continuation are reduced.

Short-term traders have just experienced a sharp short-covering rally. Price momentum is higher. Additionally, the all-time high is visible.

The "p" formation is market-generated information. Mind the MGI.

There is no meaningful excess on the daily high.

3. The break in the H and I periods left no excess on the daily low – two back-to-back, non-excess lows.

   Following the non-excess low, K period rallied to new highs.

   The pullback in L period was too sharp for there to be more than short-term buying. This is an important nuance to observe. It is only a single data point, but combined with the other information discussed above, the odds were against reaching the all-time high.
4. Failing to reach the all-time high, late liquidation ended the session. Once again, short-term traders trapped themselves.

The definition of insanity is doing the same thing over and over and expecting different results.

—Albert Einstein

CHAPTER TWENTY-SIX

BEYOND PRICE: UNVEILING MARKET DYNAMICS

Many traditional technical analysts would have you believe that price is the sole determinant of market movements. But if price were truly everything, why would anyone need to consider entry and exit points?

The foundation of market-generated information lies in three fundamental components: *price*, which presents opportunities; *time*, which governs these opportunities; and *volume*, which gauges the productiveness of these opportunities. It is the *intricate interplay* of these components – across market timeframes – that underscores the significance of price in the short term.

Short-term trading, as distinct from long-term investing, is a strategic game in which knowing your competitors is key. The competitive nature of this game is obvious when you watch your adversaries attempting to gain an advantage – which I witnessed in abundance during my early exchange memberships on the Chicago Board of Trade and the Chicago Board Options Exchange.

Price dynamics aren't always straightforward in short-term trading. Market participants often obscure their true intentions, making it challenging to discern exactly who initiated any given price action. Long-term players go to great lengths to hide intentions that would alert short-term traders, causing them to front-run their orders.

Identifying forces driving price changes is crucial for gaining a competitive edge.

Let's begin by analyzing short-term trading activity on April 2, 2024, the second day of the second quarter (Figure 26.1). The market experienced a selloff at the quarter's onset as traders sought to capitalize on the gains of the previous quarter, coupled with speculation regarding the Federal Reserve's rate adjustments – historically challenging to predict. Adding to the uncertainty, the morning of April 2 saw the release of the JOLTS report on job openings and labor turnover survey, further unsettling the market.

SELL FIRST, ASK QUESTIONS LATER

The market opened significantly lower, with heightened volatility on April 2 exacerbating the downward pressure on prices. Assessing fair value and executing trades at desired prices is exceedingly challenging under these types of conditions. Liquidity dwindled as traders hesitated to enter opposing buy orders amidst all the uncertainty. This lack of liquidity amplified downward price momentum.

Figure 26.1 The Profile on the Morning of April 2, 2024

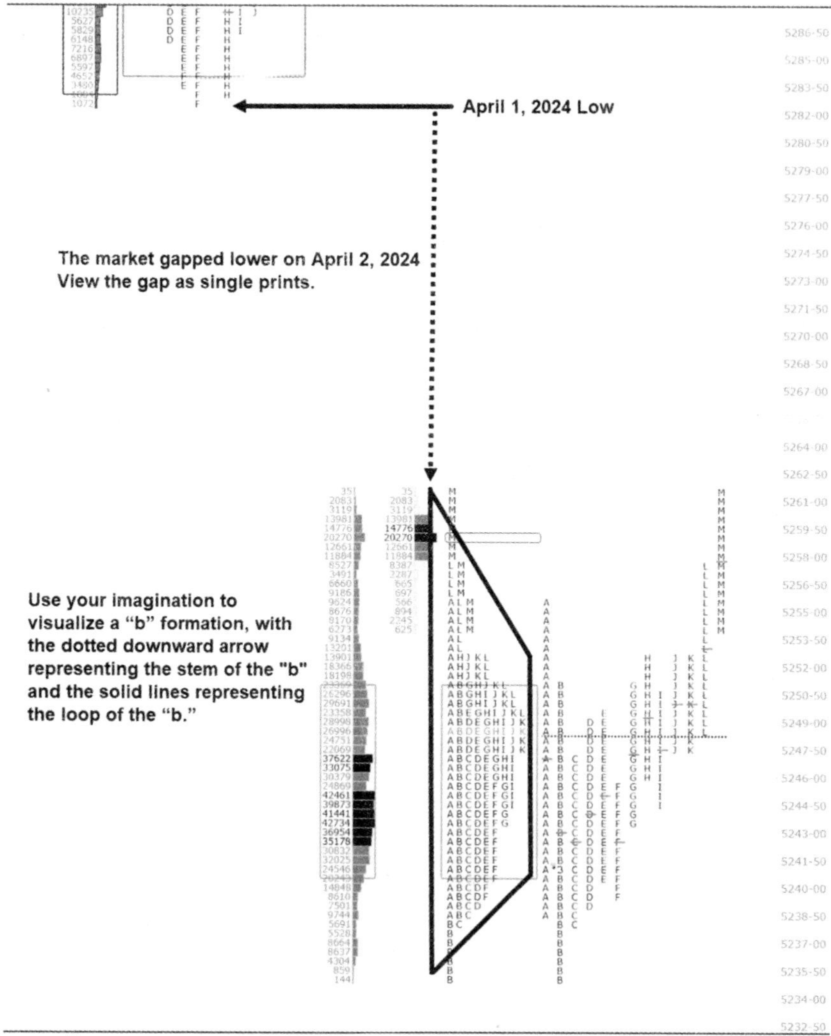

To mitigate risk, bid-ask spreads widened considerably, intensifying the downward price spiral. Emotional responses from inexperienced traders – particularly day and very short-term traders – were exacerbated by volatility, and contributed to market inefficiencies; their reactions further compounded existing flaws in the auction process.

Given these conditions, it's conceivable that the market became excessively short during early day-timeframe trading.

Examining the events of April 2, it's evident that market structure aligns with the aforementioned discussion. This knowledge can provide a significant short-term trading advantage.

The high of the dotted arrow in Figure 26.1 represents the top of the gap on April 2. Use your imagination to visualize a "**b**" formation, with the dotted downward arrow representing the stem and the solid lines representing the loop of the "**b**."

As a reminder, this structure increases the odds that short-term inventory has become dangerously short. If you only consider price, in this circumstance, then you're more likely to expect additional selling. Reviewing price *in context* conveys a more cautious perspective.

This structure is not new to you; however, the circumstances are not the same. Additionally, the late afternoon price action is deceptive.

ALL-TIME HIGH

The all-time high occurred at 5,333.50 during the Globex trading hours on March 31. While there's nothing written that says an all-time high can't occur overnight, from my observation it would be a rarity for this high to last very long. This is simply a single data point, but it does decrease the odds of downside continuation.

Taking this thinking one step further, *the manner* in which the all-time high was made decreased the odds that a resulting change in trend would occur. In other words, the long-term trend remained up.

Many experts advocate for a linear learning approach, starting with foundational concepts. Following this "rote learning," they suggest acquiring practical experience. Most recommend deferring the study of nuances until later stages.

I find this advice to be impractical, particularly in fields like trading in which delaying attention to nuance can result in significant financial losses during the learning process.

The action of short-term traders during the afternoon of April 2 underscores an important nuance. On that morning, the market experienced a sharp downward gap. As the afternoon progressed, a significant portion of day-timeframe traders – constrained by limited capital for overnight positions – rushed to cover their shorts. Despite appearing weak throughout the session, the market revealed its short inventory imbalance in I period, briefly dipping below the half-level before buyers swiftly intervened (Figure 26.2).

Successful short-term trading is highly dependent upon *paying attention to the market.* Had you not been paying close attention, it's unlikely that you would have noticed the aggressiveness of the buying below half-back. I continually advise traders to limit their focus to trading – and trading alone – while the market is open.

Ordinarily, matching J and K lows might signal weak buying. In this nuanced scenario, however, these matching lows likely resulted from nervous shorts seeking an opportunity to cover. Failure to discern this distinction could have led you to short the subsequent rally, exposing yourself to potential losses.

This afternoon exemplifies the deceptive nature of markets and underscores the importance of recognizing nuanced experiences in order to navigate them effectively.

Figure 26.2 The Profile on the Afternoon of April 1, 2024

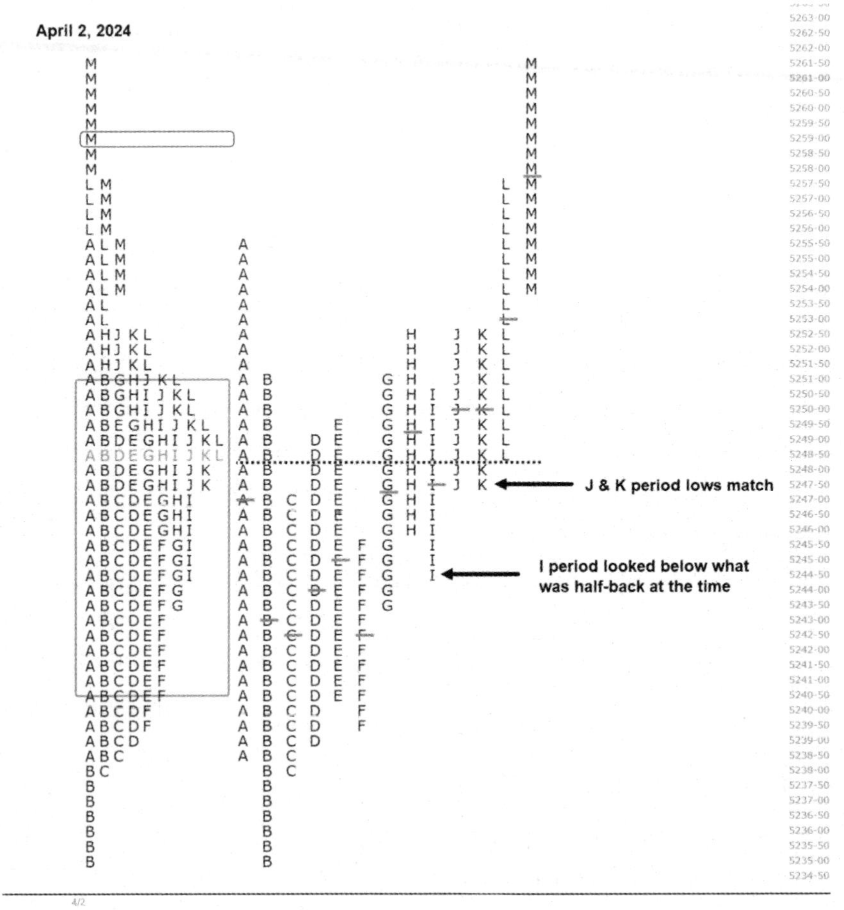

April 2, 2024

J & K period lows match

I period looked below what was half-back at the time

WHO'S IN CONTROL OF THE MARKET?

In every competitive endeavor, considerable time and effort are expended on assessing the strengths and weaknesses of the competition. The better you understand your adversaries, the higher your chances of success.

Short-term traders who overlook the competitive landscape put themselves at a serious disadvantage.

Viewing the market through the lens of the daily bar unveils a telling narrative. It appeared competitors were exhibiting a herd mentality, mindlessly driving prices downwards. The distinctive "**b**" formation in Figure 26.3 strongly suggested a surge in short-term selling activity. If there had been a mix of selling timeframes in play, the Profile would likely have displayed greater elongation.

Engage your imagination and contemplate the significance of a more symmetrical Profile, versus an overly elongated one. A symmetrical Profile would imply a diverse range of sellers across various timeframes, highlighting the probability of continued downward pressure. Conversely, an excessively elongated Profile would hint at emotionally driven selling, leading to an unusually short inventory. Both the "**b**" formation and the overly elongated Profile suggest accumulated short inventory.

Think of these Profiles like the tale of Goldilocks and the three bears: *too much, too little, just right.*

To safeguard yourself from getting swept up in the herd – while simultaneously leveraging your recognition that the herd is in motion – it's essential to maintain a balanced perspective. This involves staying attuned to market dynamics, but not blindly following the crowd.

An understanding of "too much, too little, and just right" can only be gained through active experience, and you must constantly weigh these indicators against overall market context. For example, these kinds of identifiers will vary depending on if you're in a trending or rotational market and will also be influenced by overall market volatility. While I don't particularly like the VIX (CBOE volatility index), I pay attention to it relative to the discussion above.

Up to this point we have used specific examples to demonstrate the complexity of the market. In Chapter 27 we'll focus on references to enhance your ability to identify whom you're competing against, and your ability to gauge the strength or weakness of the current auction.

Figure 26.3 The Surge in Short-Term Selling Activity

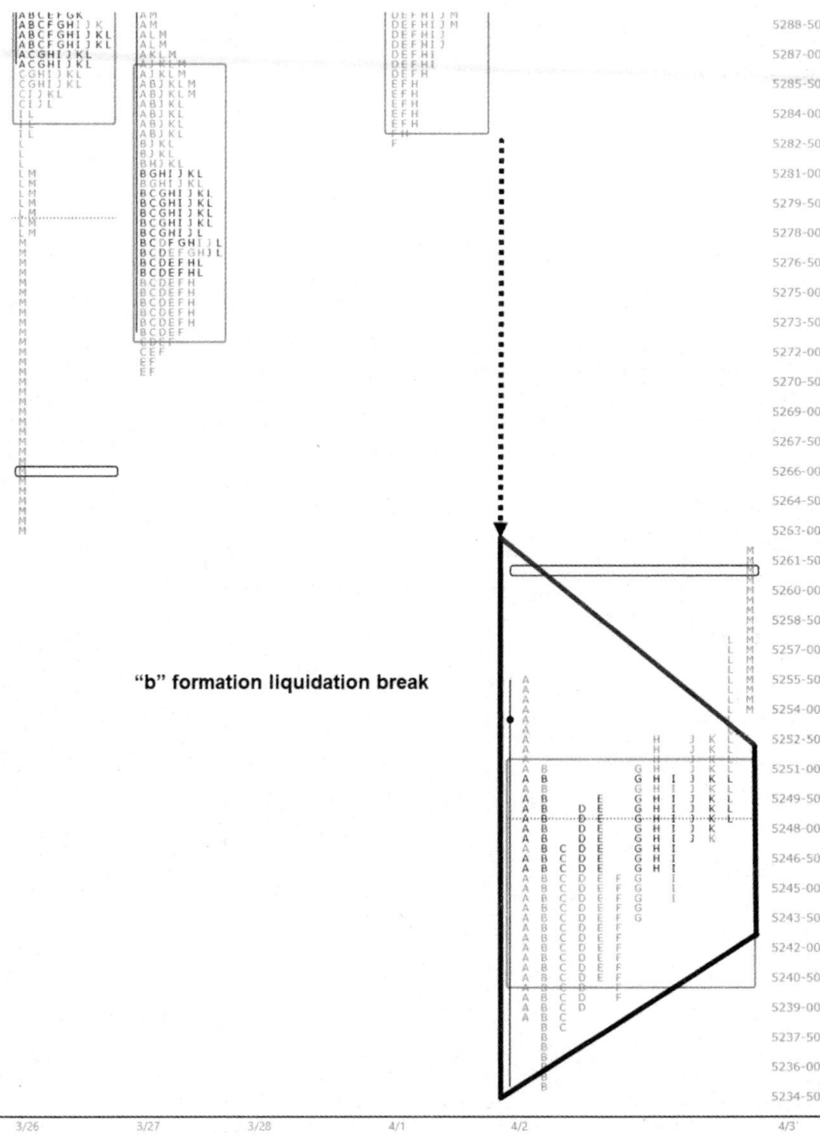

In her book *The Biggest Bluff*, Maria Konnikova asked thousands of people to play a simulated stock market game – with real financial rewards – as part of her doctoral research at Columbia. What she found was completely unexpected:

Over and over, people would overestimate the degree of control they had over events—smart people, people who excelled at many things, people who should have known better. Not only would they decide ahead of time how they were going to divide their investments, but they would decide based on incredibly limited information which stock was "good" and stick to their guns – even as they started losing money. The more they overestimated their own skill relative to luck, the less they learned from what the environment was trying to tell them, and the worse their decisions became: The participants grew increasingly less likely to switch to winning stocks, instead doubling down on losers. Because they thought they knew more than they did, they ignored any signs to the contrary – especially when, as inevitably happens in real stock markets, winners became losers and vice versa. In other words, the illusion of control is what prevented real control from emerging – and before long, the quality of people's decisions deteriorated. They did what worked in the past, or what they had decided would work – and failed to grasp that the circumstances had shifted so that a previously successful strategy was no longer so. People failed to see what the world was telling them when that message wasn't one they wanted to hear.

CHAPTER TWENTY-SEVEN

THE OPENING ENGAGEMENT STARTS HERE

Welcome to the final chapters of our journey through the world of short-term trading. We're now going to enter the dynamic arena where theory meets practice: **live trading**. Here, the concepts we've explored come to life as we immerse ourselves in the exhilarating and often unpredictable landscape of the trading session.

This is where true learning begins, as engagement and participation provide the fertile ground for honing skills, sharpening instincts, and navigating shifting market currents. On this final leg of our journey, the art of trading unfolds before our eyes.

I'm reminded of the quote from the philosopher Heraclitus: "You cannot step into the same river twice." This captures the ever-changing reality of short-term trading, reminding us that we can't understand the totality of something by limiting our attention to isolated portions.

Hector the Collector, toting years of useless baggage, won't survive this kind of engagement with the market.

The following quote provides a crucial principle of short-term trading, and it's where we'll begin our final journey.

> In the long run, prioritization beats efficiency.
>
> —**James Clear,** *Atomic Habits*

Remember this fundamental truth: **Markets are inherently irregular.** They do not adhere to predictable patterns or logical sequences. This irregularity – stemming from factors like inventory imbalances, unexpected earnings or economic releases, unforeseen announcements, interpretations of Federal Reserve statements deviating from expectations, and so forth – underscores the need for adaptability and flexibility in our trading strategies.

Throughout the book, we have written about the power, peril, and potential of habits. Now let's discuss how you can build *positive* habits. Initially, this process is time-consuming. But as the habit forms, it will become more and more comfortable, streamlined, informational, and ultimately rewarding.

The first step in developing this habit is to gain an objective perspective of the market by reviewing monthly, weekly, and daily bars, and of course daily Market Profiles. You want to first determine if the market is trending or bracketing. All bars pointing in the same direction will confirm a fully trending market.

Daily volatility often obscures broader market trends, leading to directional uncertainty. Examining the monthly bar – followed by a detailed review of the weekly bar – offers a more comprehensive perspective. In particular, the weekly bar for March–April 2024 shown in Figure 27.1 reveals the market transitioning into a short-term balance.

Another refresher: **Markets rarely exhibit sudden, dramatic shifts in direction.** Instead, they tend to undergo a balancing process. In the above

Figure 27.1 The Weekly Bar Chart, March–April 2024

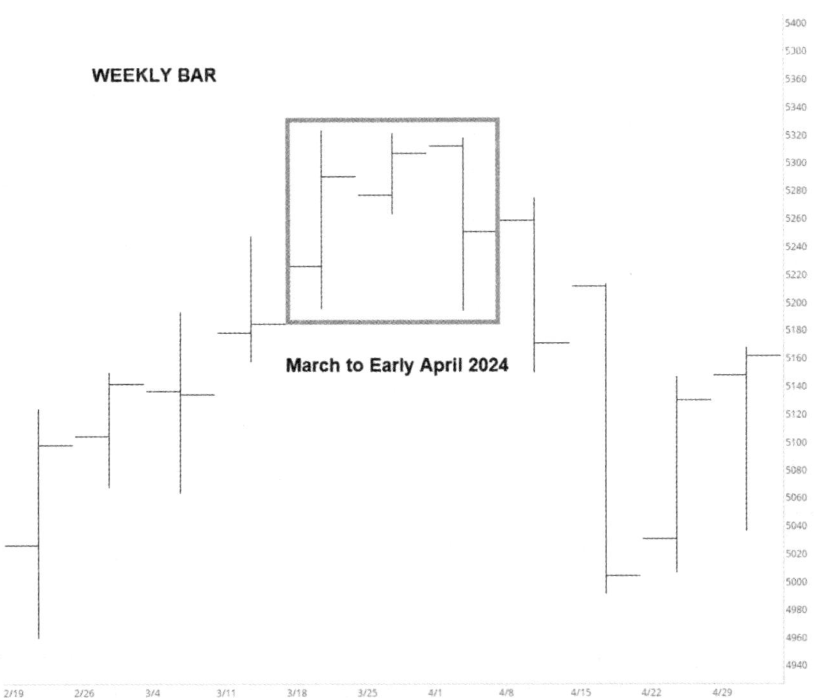

scenario, the market remained in a state of balance for four weeks before experiencing a directional shift manifested by a breakout from that balance.

Frequently, the most significant opportunities for short-term traders arise during these kinds of breakouts, which communicate a shift in market sentiment. Being a successful short-term trader is difficult unless you capitalize on a few larger opportunities.

The graphic in Figure 27.2 represents the daily bar chart for the four weeks shown in the weekly bar chart in Figure 27.1.

When no direction appears in the daily bars, I recommend you come in and go home flat (no position) each session. This allows you to maintain an open mind and react to what the market presents during the following

Figure 27.2 The Daily Bar Chart for the Four Weeks, March–April, 2024

session. Too often we get emotionally trapped by what we *want* or *need* to happen, and we may get swayed by some expert or technician.

When markets are balancing – establishing a trading range – more information is required before embarking on the next directional auction. We're again reminded that markets often defy prediction and logic, charting their own course. This is compounded as the market seeks balance.

A vital component of the "good habit" we seek to develop is a mental reminder of the importance of remaining adaptable, vigilant, and open to the unforeseen. The force of habit is the tendency to do something so frequently it becomes automatic.

CAPITALIZING ON A BREAKOUT (CHANGE IN SENTIMENT)

As the market presents you with a potential breakout from balance, remember the balance-trading guidelines:

1. Go with a breakout from balance.
2. Fade (go against) a breakout from balance that fails. On a breakout failure, the market can reverse back to the opposite extreme.

The graphic in Figure 27.3 shows a successful breakout, which is often the beginning of a trend. When a market is trending, it's seeking a new equilibrium, or a level at which two-sided trade occurs. Trading is a business. No business is successful unless two-sided trade is occurring.

Transitioning from the structured rhythm of preparation to the dynamic world of execution is by far the most emotional and challenging time for everyone. It's the moment when analysis, planning, preparation, and anticipation converge into *action*.

Execution demands presence, adaptability, and discipline.

Whether I intend to act on the opening immediately or later in the session, the period surrounding the market's opening is extremely informational; the tone for the day is frequently foreshadowed during this initial phase.

The downside breakout shown in Figure 27.3 demonstrates the maximum challenge facing short-term traders. The first exploration below the balance attracted buyers, with the market opening back within the balance during the following session.

Figure 27.3 Two-Sided Trading after Downside Breakout from Balance

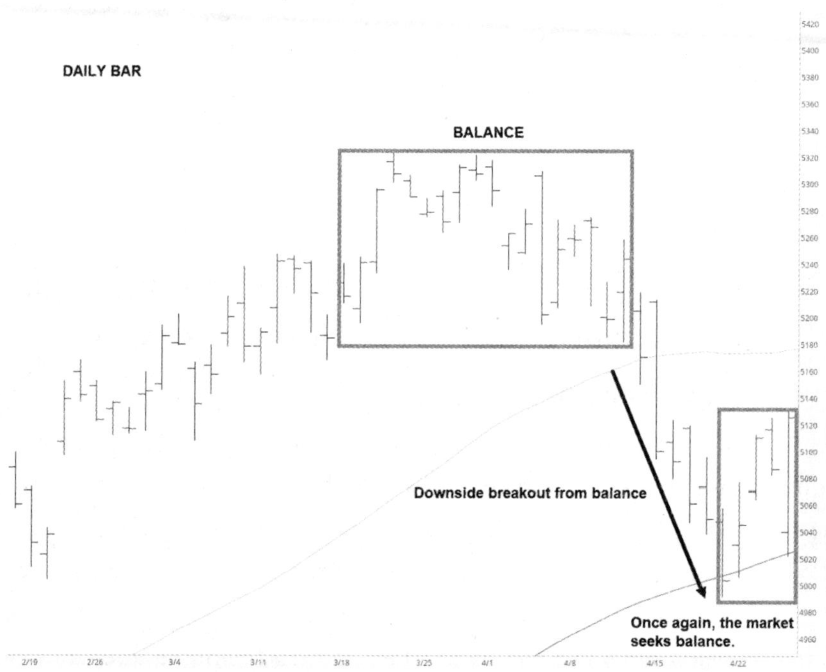

NUANCE MATTERS

Note how the peak on April 12 in Figure 27.4 closely aligned with the half-back of the previous trading session (indicated by arrow A). The precise selling from this level strongly implies it was driven by participants who had shorter timeframe horizons and weaker positions. It's improbable that more seasoned or longer-term sellers would consider the midpoint of the previous day. Executions such as selling here at precise levels resemble a "tell" akin to poker, revealing your competitors' characteristics and inclinations. Those with shorter horizons often display emotionally driven herd

Figure 27.4 The Profile for April 12, 2024

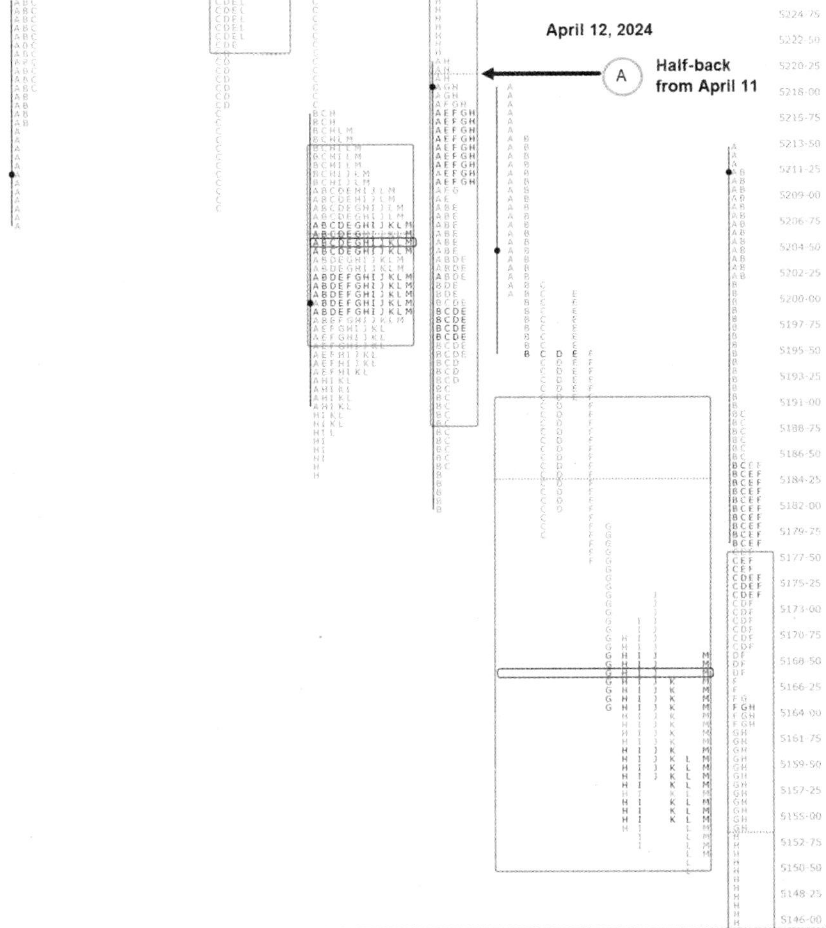

behavior that tends toward extremes. In this instance, there's a likelihood that these short-term traders (prone to extremes) will continue selling until inventory becomes too short.

On the surface this profile looks like a double distribution day. Let's dig deeper into the nuances. A closer look at the Profile – spanning from

H period through the close in M period – indicates tightly clustered activity resembling the letter "**b**" with the stem in periods A through G. Some of you might say this is not the classic "**b**" shape, but remember trading is an art. As you recall, this configuration strongly indicates long liquidation, rather than a more forceful blend of long liquidation and new selling activity. Once this pattern emerges, the likelihood of a short-covering rally rises significantly.

The market opened sharply higher on the following session and immediately sold off, confirming the downside breakout. (Often inexperienced traders are misguided by overnight trade/overnight inventory.) Understanding your competition and staying one step ahead are part of the many unique challenges that short-term traders face. Once the short inventory from the 12th was rebalanced, the downside breakout continued, but prudent short-term traders would have covered their shorts on that day (April 12). There was too much uncertainty to remain long in the face of the short inventory.

Only with extensive experience can you begin to successfully operate in this competitive, volatile environment.

Monitoring for continuation is a highly recommended practice once a trade has been initiated – though many wonder exactly what that entails. The answer to that question is "ongoing" as conditions continually change. In the current example, however, if you were short on April 12, it would have been prudent to cover positions as the prospects for continuation were unfavorable.

A TREND IS IN MOTION

The breakout from balance signals the initiation of a downward trend. Once a trend is established, the market is once again seeking balance, which offers the greatest opportunity for two-way trade.

Given that each trader operates on a different timeframe, the interpretation of what constitutes a trend varies widely. To add additional complexity, countertrends can occur within longer-term trends, contributing to the sustainability of the overarching trend.

The perception of "trend" depends on the trader.

During my daily preparation, I focus on both longer-term trends and the subtler trends within them, including countertrends. The daily and weekly bars are most relevant when identifying shorter-term trends.

Remember, we are in the process of crafting a powerful habit. Stay mindful of the journey as we delve into specifics. The goal is to build a routine that not only sharpens your trading skills but nurtures your growth as a trader. Think of it as developing stepping stones toward your successful future.

BALANCING FOR ALL TIMEFRAMES

Earlier, we approached balance from a longer-timeframe perspective. Like so many of the concepts we've discussed, "balance" is applicable from the shortest to the longest timeframes. My shortest timeframe begins with a 30-minute inside bar, followed by two or more overlapping bars. As you can imagine, an inside day (trading entirely within the previous day's range) is a slightly longer period of balance.

Balance can continue with multiple overlapping days, weeks, or even months. Inside weeks or months of course also represent balance of a longer-term nature. The importance of focusing on balance is that an *exit* from balance indicates a change in market tenor.

There is no opportunity unless change is occurring.

While everything must be viewed within context, and recognizing that trading is more art than science, the overall guidelines remain: *Go with a breakout from balance and fade a failed breakout.*

Balance also plays a significant role when we're monitoring for continuation, as the market seeks the range where the greatest amount of two-sided trade can occur. If I have been in a directional trade and the market begins to balance, I will strongly consider flattening my position.

As we complete this trading session, the important observations to ponder are the formation of balance areas and identifying when the market is exiting from balance, which indicates change – where opportunity hides.

MARKETS ALWAYS HANDLE CURRENT BUSINESS FIRST

In this section, we'll review the impact that economic releases and other announcements – along with overnight inventory – can have on price.

First, let's consider the implications of economic releases. Over the years I have consistently advised clients to be prepared for all scheduled releases, knowing exactly when they're to be announced. I also advise *against* reading these releases. Similar to reading a prospectus or offering circular, the really relevant information is often buried in a footnote. In economic releases and other such announcements, it's often either the revision to the prior report or a component of the release that proves to be most significant.

Many inexperienced traders read only the headline, increasing the odds that they're operating on insufficient information. Temporary distortions are often created as shorter-term traders tend to act first and think later. These emotional reactions often lead to sharply over- or underpriced moments.

Approximately 75% of the time, there's a counter-auction, or partial counter-auction, relative to overnight inventory. We measure overnight inventory relative to the settle (the official price published by the exchange). It's not uncommon for overnight trade to continue in the direction last witnessed during NYSE trading hours if you're considering the equity indices. It is far more difficult to make this assessment relative to other markets.

When I initially introduced this concept and its relevance to day-timeframe trading, it faced criticism from larger professional traders who argued that overnight volume wasn't sufficient to merit attention. However, this skepticism precisely underscores the importance of the issue: Roughly 75% of the time, overnight moves lack substantial volume support, leading to a counter-auction.

One of the most common mistakes made by short-term traders is misinterpreting this counter-auction as indicative of a more enduring directional move. An example of this is when overnight inventory is heavily long and there's an immediate liquidation when the market opens. However, the selling pressure is quickly rebuffed and the market rallies for the remainder of the session.

EARLY TRADE/OVERNIGHT INVENTORY

I have often heard educators and advisors tell traders not to engage the market during the first hour. This is poor advice as a blanket statement. What occurs during the opening minutes often sets the tone for the remainder of the day.

I'm frequently asked, "*How do you know if this is going to be a trend day?*"

You don't. However, early trade often alerts you to the possibility – if it's going to be a trend day, market confidence is usually high from the opening.

How the market reacts to overnight inventory often sets the stage for the day. For example, earlier we observed that approximately 75% of the time there's a counter-auction relative to overnight inventory. If there is *no* counter-auction, the odds are high that the market will continue in the direction of overnight trade.

For example, if overnight inventory is long and there's no counter-auction or correction, the odds favor a strong market to the upside. Likewise, if overnight inventory is short and there is no counter-auction, the odds favor a strong day to the downside. In both examples, trend days are more likely.

But it's rarely that simple. Constantly remain aware of other expected announcements or events.

If there are high-odds counter-auctions, the outcomes tend to be more varied. Additionally, *where* the market opens can be revealing. For example, if the market opens approximately centered in the previous day's range, there is no meaningful change. Under these circumstances, market chop is highly likely. A prudent trader will patiently wait for a clearer opportunity. Getting "caught in the chop" often leads to the loss of both psychological and financial capital.

Psychological capital can be the most expensive.

WHAT IS THE MARKET ATTEMPTING TO DO?

The Market Profile, as a distribution curve, serves as a fundamental tool in organizing the continuous two-way auction process of the market, facilitating our visualization of its ever-changing dynamics. At its core lies the concept of *value*. Value encapsulates roughly one standard deviation, or about 70% of the day's activity. Focusing on developing value empowers us to monitor the evolving market more effectively.

Within the constant maze of auctions and counter-auctions, vigilant monitoring of *developing value* assists us in pinpointing the most probable market direction for the day.

Monitoring for *continuation* requires a closer look at developing value. For example, an overly elongated Profile suggests highly emotional activity; a truncated Profile demonstrates a low level of interest. Or like Goldilocks and the three bears, activity may be *just right*. It is only through extended experience that the significance of this paragraph becomes appreciated. This is what engagement is about.

Volume – which measures the success or failure of market activity – is also relevant. Higher prices on *decreasing* volume reduce the odds of continuation, as higher prices on *increasing* volume increase the odds of continuation.

(As you gain experience, you'll understand that this is more complex than stated.)

MORE NUANCES

We're going to cover one more major topic that helps isolate who we're competing against during any given period.

Though first, let's acknowledge that the reality of successful trading remains in the distance for most. In endeavors marked by intense competition and demanding performance standards, the guidance provided in "how-to" books merely scratches the surface. These resources can serve as a gateway to the subject matter, rewarding a nascent interest, but mastery and true understanding can only be achieved through sustained dedication and hands-on experience.

Deeper exploration into any highly competitive domain reveals a world rich with subtleties and complexities that go far beyond the scope of instructional texts. These subtleties are often elusive, requiring a "nuanced" understanding that can only be cultivated through immersive engagement and continuous learning.

While books offer fundamental principles and techniques, they fail to capture the intricacies of *real-world application* and the dynamic nature of competitive environments. It is only through a commitment to ongoing refinement that you can begin to grasp the finer points that separate dreamers from consistently successful traders.

Mastery in such endeavors is not simply about following a set of prescribed steps outlined in a book; it's about developing a profound understanding of the underlying principles in play, honing one's skill through relentless practice, and adapting to the ever-evolving challenges that define the competitive landscape. It's a layer-by-layer experience where losses and successes contribute to the depth of your expertise.

COMPETITORS

My understanding of the importance of identifying your competition was initially sparked during my time on the floor of the Chicago Board of Trade. There, I observed the origins of large trading desk orders, often communicated through hand signals. While orders from retail firms typically garnered minimal attention, those from heavyweights like Goldman Sachs commanded substantial interest.

Transitioning away from the trading floor provided me with a new perspective. Major institutional investment firms frequently circulated orders among various entries. If the order was shared with multiple firms, those left out quickly figured it out and anticipated its impact during the session. I recall observing a savvy institutional trading manager who, realizing he wouldn't receive the shared order, instructed his desk to purchase assets he knew would be in demand once the shared order entered the market.

Understanding the source and timing of business flows remains crucial. Broadly, I aim to discern whether orders primarily originate from institutions or individuals. Institutions typically exhibit greater patience and endurance, with their orders unfolding gradually, making them less likely to prompt immediate responses. The gradualness of institutional order flow can last for extensive periods. Conversely, individual orders are more susceptible to emotional influences and rapid reversals.

Knowing the difference is crucial to your chances of success.

DISTINGUISHING BETWEEN COMPETITORS

I categorized competitors based on two main criteria. First, when trading activity remains concentrated around precise levels – such as the previous day's high or low, the opening price, half-back from the previous day or overnight, and half-back of 30-minute bars – it's likely driven by short-term traders. In such cases, detailed analysis often ends there.

Conversely, when the aforementioned levels are largely overlooked, it indicates engagement with longer timeframes.

Few short-term or day-timeframe traders recognize the significance of this distinction. Can you imagine playing a tennis match and not observing if your opponent is left- or right-handed?

CHAPTER TWENTY-EIGHT

THE POWER OF A WELL-KEPT JOURNAL

When I was introduced to the Market Profile as an organizing tool, it opened my mind to how markets distribute bids and offers via a continuous two-way auction process. But the introduction also included what I consider to be the most important formula for successful trading:

Market Understanding + Self Understanding + Strategy = Success

An improved understanding of the markets was almost immediate – but that improvement was not correlated with financial success, and I continued to slide backward. As I have frequently shared in my ongoing educational programs, I was unprofitable as a trader for more than 20 years.

Market understanding that is not accompanied by an advancement in understanding the *self* does not lead to profitability. Self-understanding can be brutal, as we're forced to confront how we really act, as opposed to the mental picture we create of ourselves.

To get past the hurdle of self-delusion, you must embrace the habit of journaling, exposing your innermost thoughts, fears, and selfish urges, recording them along with your trading decisions to begin to rub away at the fogged window of self-understanding. Journaling by itself won't enhance your trading, but it is a starting point for recognizing your emotional traps and deeply ingrained biases.

That's when the real work begins.

If you're considering journaling, it's worth reflecting on some of the insights I've shared earlier in this book. Many traders have undergone educational programs emphasizing reversion-to-the-mean trades. However, my observations over the years suggest that markets move too swiftly for this strategy to reliably succeed.

Similarly, strategies relying on confirmation tend to be unproductive due to market pace. Roughly 15% of trading days exhibit strong trends, making the concept of "waiting for confirmation" extremely challenging. Success as a short-term trader often depends on capturing a high percentage of these trend days.

Surprisingly, Tom Hougaard's book *Best Loser Wins* revealed that short-term traders have more winning than losing trades. But here's the rub: The average win is smaller than the average loss. It's vital to track your ability to let profits run and examine whether emotions are influencing your decisions. We've noticed a strong tendency among unsuccessful traders to take profits too early.

Can you recognize when the odds suggest that market inventory has become dangerously too long or too short?

Can you resist the temptation to listen to market commentators, and instead act on market-generated information? Listening to these "experts" often introduces cognitive dissonance, clouding your judgment and hindering short-term trading decisions.

YOU ARE YOUR MARKET

The most important market day traders need to understand is themselves. Each trader must design a journal process that is consistent with their personal makeup. The items I consider most essential are:

- **Emotional control:** Can you manage emotions like fear, greed, and frustration to avoid impulsive trading?
- **Risk tolerance:** How comfortable are you with potential losses? Are you prone to fear of missing out (FOMO) or fear of losing? (I suspect this is the biggest issue.)
- **Discipline:** Can you enter and exit positions even when emotions are high?
- **Analytical skills:** Have you properly prepared, so you're able to make adjustments under pressure?
- **Decision-making:** Can you think clearly under pressure and make quick, informed decisions?

The challenge before you is to answer these questions – thoroughly and honestly – and use those insights to design your own personal process, so you can avoid the constant pitfalls of wishful thinking and risk aversion and a dozen other perils in order to be fully present for what is actually happening in the unfolding complexity of the market.

JOURNALING IS PREPARATION

"Journaling" and "preparation" might appear to be separate endeavors, but they're part of the same holistic process of developing a positive, productive practice. Carefully noting circumstances and emotional states experienced before, during, and after every trade will help you see patterns, so you can better focus your attention and improve your odds of success.

When you write something down, you are *telling a story*. And the story you tell exerts a powerful influence on your decision-making systems. If you follow a regular process of recording the truth of your immediate experience, you can begin to avoid being unduly swayed by opinions influenced by emotions.

Create a new routine and record your preparation methods and mental states before the market opens. Hold yourself accountable. Pay close attention and you will learn to avoid common biases like confusing *short-term trading* with *investing*. When you record your objectives, time horizon, and strategies, your habits will come into clearer focus, empowering you to avoid traps like FOMO. *When do you tend to be susceptible to these feelings? How do they influence your trading? How do you respond emotionally when you miss a big move?*

Observe your emotions as you trade. Investigate how your ability to reason gets hampered by feelings. Pay attention to how pundits, "experts," and news can disrupt your trading strategy.

Recognizing emotional impulses helps you avoid throwing good money after bad.

Trading during volatile periods is a challenge for even the most emotionally mature traders. Many of the most successful discretionary traders I've come to know have no problem stepping aside when volatility results in emotional turmoil. Let the market clarify itself before you resume trading to avoid the loss of financial capital, and perhaps more importantly, to minimize the loss of *emotional* capital, which can be crippling.

Don't give up on preparation when the results aren't immediately apparent. Do the work, be patient, and in time you will see results. As we quoted earlier, "*Our biggest weakness is not recognizing our own weakness.*" Keeping a detailed trade journal will help you minimize the inevitable shortcomings that everyone suffers, now and then.

In closing, I'm pleased to share some final thoughts from Brett Steenbarger, a clinical psychologist and trader who has published numerous articles and books on trading psychology, whose counsel and friendship have been invaluable through the years.

THE PSYCHOLOGY OF KEEPING TRADING JOURNALS

Brett Steenbarger

What is the essential function of a trading journal? No, it's not to vent frustrated emotions, and it's also not to passively record P/L and actions taken during the day, week, or month.

At its best, a trading journal is a way of talking to yourself. It's a means for you, the observer, to talk with you, the trader. In a very real sense, we are our own trading analysts. We are always talking to ourselves. The question is whether we're truly providing actionable information with our self-talk. Trading journals turn routine self-talk into constructive talk.

The opposite of trading reactively and emotionally is trading *consciously*, with full awareness of what we're doing and why we're doing it. Good trading is necessarily mindful trading and purposeful trading. When we talk to ourselves constructively, we focus ourselves on opportunity and purpose. In that sense, trading journals guide our self-awareness.

We can identify two purposes for trading journals: previewing and reviewing.

Previewing

Previewing represents our preparation for upcoming trading. We scan charts and displays of information, such as the Market Profile. We read research reports, track breaking news, and speak with knowledgeable colleagues. We conduct studies of relevant market history and investigate how markets related to ours are behaving and why. We analyze and analyze and we draw upon the trading journal to collect our thoughts and also to think about our thinking. Psychologists call this "metacognition."

As we collect pieces of the market puzzle, we start to assemble those pieces to detect a larger picture. The role of the trading journal is to collect all our puzzle pieces, so that we can make sense of what is going on. This is the essence of what portfolio managers call "idea generation," and it's a fundamentally creative process. We can't hope to hold all information in our minds all the time. The trading journal collects our thoughts and observations so that we can begin the process of metacognition. It is a way we brainstorm and generate fresh market and trading perspectives.

Why is this important?

If we don't generate fresh market perspectives, we are going to be locked into consensus thinking. So often, profitability is found in detecting where the herd is wrong. The trading journal previews markets so that we can generate ideas that differentiate us from the crowd.

We sometimes hear that success in trading is all about maintaining a positive mindset. That is only partly true. Without unique, differentiated ideas, there can be no distinguished returns. Mindset is necessary to success in performance endeavors, but it is never sufficient. When we use a trading journal to preview the trading day or week and identify fresh opportunity, we actually help to create a constructive, positive mindset.

But there is a second function of trading journals. We can use journals not only to preview opportunity, but to *review performance*.

Reviewing

When we journal about our trading performance, we make detailed observations of what we did well and what we could have done better. These observations form the basis for very specific trading goals. Our goals can be to repeat and expand what we have done well, and our goals can be to improve what we didn't do well. In review mode, the trading journal is a framework for self-observation. It is a mirror for viewing all that we've done, so that we can approach future trading purposefully.

Effective trading journals that review performance don't stop at setting goals. Rather, they translate goals into specific plans for improvement. Perhaps I sized a position too large due to an overconfidence bias. My goal is to make sure I size positions in line with my risk objectives. My plans for doing so involve following specific formulas that translate how much I'm willing to bet on ideas into proper trade sizes based upon the volatility of the instrument I'm trading, the correlation of the trade with other positions I may have on, and where I set a rational stop level for the trade.

In many cases, the plan that emerges from our trading journal's observations and goals is a process. We create robust processes that can be internalized as positive habit patterns – and that drive ever-improving results.

Reviewing performance, setting goals and plans, and implementing our changes going forward are known in psychology as *deliberate practice*. A wealth of research in psychology shows us that there is a very close relationship between the consistency of our deliberate practice and the acquisition of expert performance. The trading journal structures our observations of ourselves and helps us translate those observations into purposeful improvement.

We started by observing that trading journals are structured methods for talking to ourselves. In preview mode, journals focus our attention on market-related information and prepare us for unique trading opportunities. In review mode, journals help us examine ourselves and learn from both our strengths and our vulnerabilities.

Successful traders are always working on market understanding.

Successful traders are always working on themselves.

Take a look at your trading journal. Are you finding unique opportunities? Are you developing yourself uniquely? Would you hire a trader who came to an interview with your trading journal?

Effective trading journals reveal you at your best. Novelist-philosopher Ayn Rand observed that anyone who fights for tomorrow lives in it today. Your journal helps you live in your future.

Many of the things you can count, don't count. Many of the things you can't count, really count.

—Albert Einstein

CHAPTER TWENTY-NINE

THAT'S A WRAP

This is being written on May 15, 2024, following an extremely volatile market on May 14, which was a whipsaw nightmare for novices and a blessing for experienced traders. This chapter wasn't part of the original plan, but the 14th presented an ideal opportunity to weave together key themes, including tempo as a "tell." In poker, a tell refers to a shift in a player's behavior or demeanor that can hint at the strength or weakness of their hand.

Those skilled at reading tells can gain a considerable advantage.

In this final chapter, we introduce the concept of "tempo" as a tell. The tempo observed on the afternoon of the 14th alerted us to the possibility of a short-covering rally. Tempo – akin to rhythm in music – serves as a subtle yet potent indicator in navigating intricate market dynamics.

The graphic in Figure 29.1 allows you to examine May 14, including overnight trade leading up to the NYSE opening. This activity is important because it allows you to view the reaction to the producer price index (PPI) an hour prior to the NYSE opening. The PPI is used to measure the average change in U.S. wholesale prices. Its relevance on the 14th was related to the market's obsessive focus on the Federal Reserve's future rate-setting policy.

Figure 29.1 The Profile for May 14, 2024

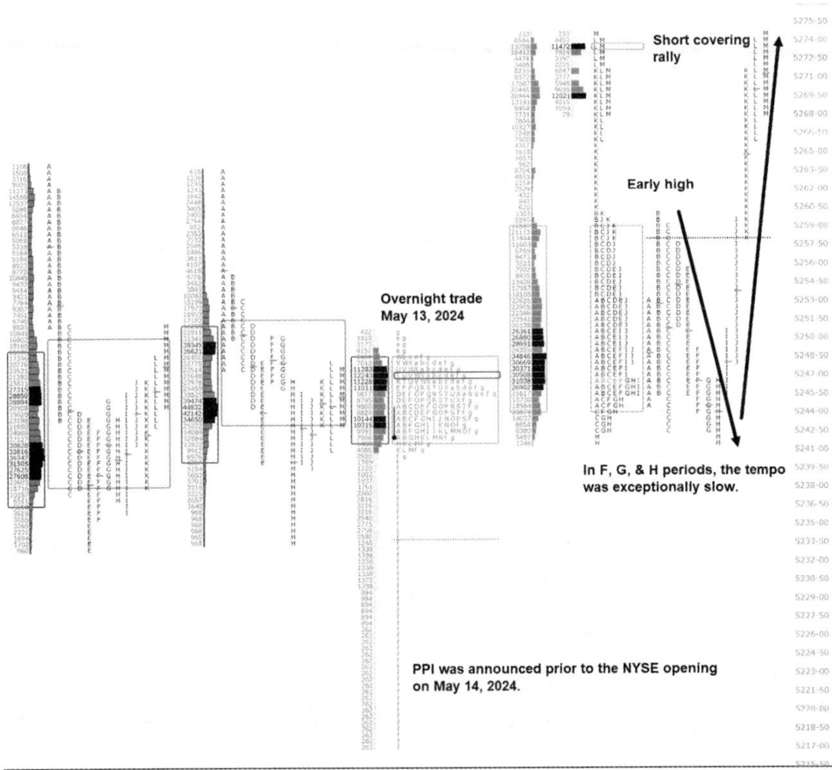

Earlier in the book, we suggested that you not read scheduled economic announcements, but rather observe the market's *reaction* to them. Our reasoning was that most of us are not equipped to fully appreciate the nuances of these types of announcements. Short-term traders tend to react to the headline in a herd-like fashion, without appreciating revisions to previous announcements or components of the release.

In the announcement on the 14th, overnight trade incorporated a sharp spike lower as traders reacted to the headline. The rapid recovery resulted from more experienced traders reacting to more important components of the release.

Throughout the book, we have continually stressed the importance of understanding short-term inventory conditions in order to be a competitive, profitable short-term trader. Following the PPI release, a herd-like reaction to the headline led to extremely short, short-term inventory. This is visible in the sharp downward move in Figure 29.1.

Short covering and momentum buying continued through the early high in the B period. B, C, D, E, F, G, and H periods saw consistent selling. Inventory had gone from too short to too long and was in the process of becoming too short. Your question should have been: *How can you determine that it was becoming too short?*

Tempo, or "pace" on the downside, was extremely slow. Tempo is an extremely advanced concept. Tempo *with* the trend (the long-term trend we're discussing is clearly higher) and tempo *against* the trend can be significantly different.

Upward tempo with the trend is not as telling as tempo against the trend.

This statement is extremely complex and can only be understood after you have amassed considerable experience and observation. Your tendency might now be to look for tempo everywhere; introducing this concept might initially hamper your trading. Its usefulness is selective – when it's relevant, it will separate you from the herd.

In Figure 29.1, the narrowness of the range in the F, G, and H periods also signaled that the market was experiencing difficulty as it attempted to trade lower. This is obvious when you view it after the fact, but it was far more challenging in real time; for approximately 90 minutes, you witnessed the market continually trade lower.

The short-covering rally was equally challenging, as the market initially ground higher. Many traders sold into the rally, further exacerbating the short inventory. Unless you understood the initial short inventory, you could have easily fallen into the same trap. The new shorts were fueling the rally.

FINAL THOUGHTS

Throughout this book, we have delved into the essential market components of time, price, and volume, integrating them with insights into the many ways our biases, hopes, and fears influence our ability to make clear-headed decisions. The Market Profile offers a framework for assessing the complexities of market movements, providing an objective mechanism for interpreting market-generated information – your clearest window into what is actually happening in the present tense.

Your journey as a trader is just beginning – is *always* just beginning. This book was written as a foundational text, a starting point from which continuous learning and adaptation will take you on a journey uniquely your own. Markets evolve, technologies advance, and human behaviors shift; so too must your understanding and strategy.

Remember, the greatest barrier to success in trading, as in all areas of life, is ourselves. The challenge lies not only in mastering the market but in mastering the self. The journey toward self-mastery is ongoing, requiring persistence, patience, and presence.

If you take away one thing, let it be this: *engage deeply*, not just with the markets, but with your own patterns of thought and reaction. Recognize that each trading decision is a moment of self-revelation, an opportunity to learn more about the complexities of both the markets and your psyche.

I invite you to revisit the chapters, reflect on the lessons, and continue to write in the empty pages provided – not just to record strategies, but to document your evolving understanding and emotional responses. This book is designed not merely to be read, but to be used as a tool for continuous reflection and growth.

Thank you for joining me on this exploration of markets and the mind. May your trading journey be as rewarding intellectually and emotionally as it is financially. Take charge of your fate through awareness, analysis, and mindful action in the markets… and beyond.

> The past perpetuates itself through lack of presence. The quality of your consciousness at this moment is what shapes the future.
>
> —**Eckhart Tolle,** *The Power of Now*

APPENDIX A

REFERENCE DEFINITIONS

In Chapter 21, we discussed explicit and implicit learning. Defining market reference points falls under the realm of *explicit* learning, while understanding their implications constitutes *implicit* learning. Refining your implicit skills – which are crucial for success – requires that you continuously refine your ability to observe market dynamics around these key benchmarks, enhancing your analytical powers, and developing a better understanding of your competition.

Many of these reference points serve as psychological markers that guide trading decisions. When these anchors consistently draw attention, it suggests a prevalence of short-term competition. Conversely, when these references hold minimal significance, it often indicates a broader, longer-term trading environment.

Of course exceptions exist. For instance, when inventory reaches extremes – either excessively long or short – these extremes can trigger short covering or long liquidation. Traders commonly misinterpret this activity, attributing it to longer timeframes.

Here is a list of some of the more notable short-term references I've observed; those marked with an asterisk (*) are unique to my observations over the years.

- **Daily half-back:** Dynamic, as it will change with the market.
- **Excess high or low:** Identifiable in the form of at least two single prints.
- **Half-back from the prior 30-minute bar and current 30-minute bar*:** When it is obvious that traders are using this reference to make buy/sell decisions, it alerts us to the odds that this action is the result of the shortest of timeframes. While price may continue directionally, the odds of retracement are also increasing, as the shorter timeframes have less staying power.
- **Last:** The exchange officially establishes the last trade of the session.
- **Late afternoon pullback low on an upward trend day*:** Remaining above this level in the following session implies that no meaningful change has occurred. Acceptance below the late afternoon pullback low in the following session indicates change is occurring.
- **Late afternoon rally high on a downward trend day*:** Mirror image of the above.
- A **Nuance*:** A high or low could be both an excess high (single prints) and a weak high (within a single tick of a nearby previous mechanical reference).
- **Overnight half-back:** Static.
- **Overnight high or low:** Assists in recognizing change relative to overnight trade.

- **Point of Control (POC):** The fairest price at which trade is being conducted, which assists in recognizing subtle market movements.
- **Poor high or low:** No excess or single prints indicates low odds that this high/low will endure, indicating higher odds that it will be revisited.
- **Previous day's high or low:** Helps you recognize change (or lack of change).
- **Settle:** The official price set by the exchange at the end of each session – not necessarily the close. It is from this reference that change is measured in future sessions.
- **Weak high or low*:** Determined as "weak" because it is within a single tick of a recent identifiable reference, for example, the previous day's high or low, overnight high or low, or any obvious recent mechanical reference.

This list is not meant to be all-inclusive. Learning to recognize these references is explicit. When you begin to grasp their relevance, implicit learning is involved.

APPENDIX B

READING LIST

I'm a heavy reader, and over the years I've encountered several books that served as signposts on the road to developing my skills as a human being and a trader. The following synopses briefly highlight the gist of the books I've found most meaningful for developing self-awareness.

With the exception of *Grit*, I believe these books require multiple readings. I, for one, wasn't able to understand the real depth with a single read. Each time through developed a conceptual layer that allowed me to recognize more relevant information that I was able to put to use.

Like all things worthwhile, *it's a process*.

THE ART OF LEARNING BY JOSH WAITZKIN

This remarkable book follows the author's journey from chess prodigy to martial arts champion, exploring his insights into how best to master any skill. Waitzkin discusses the importance of deliberate practice, the role of resilience in the face of setbacks, and the need for adaptability. The book offers valuable strategies for continuous improvement and personal growth.

THE POWER OF HABIT BY CHARLES DUHIGG

This insightful volume explores the science behind habits and how they can be transformed. Duhigg delves into the neurological and psychological mechanisms that shape habits, both individual and collective. He presents real-life examples, from personal routines to organizational behaviors, demonstrating how habits can be changed to achieve positive outcomes. The book provides practical insights on harnessing the power of habits for personal and professional growth, emphasizing the role of cues, routines, and rewards in shaping behavior.

ATOMIC HABITS BY JAMES CLEAR

This best-seller delves into the transformative impact of small habits. Clear explores the concept of atomic habits, "tiny changes with remarkable results," and highlights the compound effect of consistent actions. The book emphasizes the role of identity in habit formation and offers practical strategies for breaking bad habits and building positive ones. Clear's approach focuses on the power of marginal gains, encouraging readers to make small adjustments to create significant, lasting change in their lives.

INCOGNITO: THE SECRET LIVES OF THE BRAIN BY DAVID EAGLEMAN

Incognito delves into the mysteries of consciousness. Eagleman explores how our brains work beneath the surface, highlighting the vast amount of processing that occurs unconsciously. He discusses the complexities of perception, decision-making, and behavior, and how these processes shape our everyday lives. The book provides a fascinating journey into the hidden workings of the mind and challenges our understanding of who we are and how we perceive the world around us.

GRIT: THE POWER OF PASSION AND PERSEVERANCE BY ANGELA DUCKWORTH

Duckworth's book explores the concept of *grit*, which she defines as a combination of passion and perseverance in the pursuit of long-term goals. She argues that talent alone is not the primary predictor of success; instead, it's one's ability to stick with and work relentlessly toward objectives that matter most. She draws on her research in psychology and real-world examples to demonstrate how grit can be cultivated, and how it plays a crucial role in achieving success in various fields – from education to business and sports. The book offers insights and practical advice on how you can develop your grit and work toward achieving your ambitions.

THE BIGGEST BLUFF BY MARIA KONNIKOVA

A captivating exploration of the world of high-stakes poker and the lessons it can teach about decision-making, probability, and psychology. Konnikova, a psychologist and writer, immerses herself in the world of professional poker, learning from masters of the game like Erik Seidel. Through her experiences, she delves into the intricacies of risk-taking, emotional control, and the balance between skill and chance. The book offers insights into human behavior and the power of strategic thinking, both at the poker table and in everyday life.

GUT FEELINGS: THE INTELLIGENCE OF THE UNCONSCIOUS BY GERD GIGERENZER

This book explores the idea that our intuition, or "gut feeling," is a valuable form of decision-making that relies on our brain's ability to process information quickly and efficiently. Gigerenzer argues that, in many situations, relying on simple rules of thumb and heuristics can lead to better decisions than overthinking or relying on complex analytical reasoning. The book explores real-world examples and research findings to demonstrate how our intuitive judgments can be surprisingly accurate and beneficial.

Gigerenzer's book also makes the point that it's a mistake to compare the mind to a computer; the brain has more and different computing power (for now). One salient example is "the gaze heuristic," which is used in directing motion to achieve a goal using a single variable. For example, when a baseball is hit high in the air, the computer power necessary to compute where the ball will land won't be complete before the ball hits the ground. However, an outfielder using the gaze heuristic simply focuses on the ball and adjusts his running speed – a totally different capability.

A similar dynamic occurs when attempting to assess the speed of the market, often referred to as "tempo." Tempo is almost impossible to teach; it must be learned in the same way an outfielder learns to catch a fly ball. This simple example helped me appreciate the potential of intuition to be a vital factor in successful trading.

THE DAILY TRADING COACH: 101 LESSONS FOR BECOMING YOUR OWN TRADING PSYCHOLOGIST BY BRETT N. STEENBARGER

This book provides traders with researched-backed methods for coaching themselves to better trading performance. Steenbarger is both a clinical psychologist and a trader, and he integrates both skills in a versatile reading experience that allows readers to explore in a non-linear fashion. This unique approach enhances the book's accessibility and ensures that readers can delve into the topics that interest them most. Practical reinforcing exercises accompany each lesson, adding to the book's compelling utility. The cost of individual professional support is prohibitive for many traders, and this book provides a self-guided path toward self-improvement.

APPENDIX C

JIM DALTON TRADING

Visit our website at jimdaltontrading.com to learn about our signature eCourses, access recordings of our public webinars, and discover more book recommendations. The goal of our educational offerings is to help you become a better trader by teaching you how to:

- Begin with a top-down approach to improve short-term trading results.
- Read and interpret the daily two-way continuous auction via the Market Profile.
- Hone your intuition – a must for proficient and expert-level traders.
- Understand and use cognitive dissonance to your advantage.
- Use repetition to your advantage – important for acquiring any skill.
- Understand the difference between developed and anchor trades.

- Recognize anomalies and understand their significance.
- Understand the importance of tempo for advanced traders.
- Recognize the signs of markets that are getting too long or too short.
- Understand odds, and more importantly, how to think in terms of odds.
- Understand the importance of what does *not* occur.
- Monitor trades for continuation.
- Let the trade come to you instead of actively seeking it out.

FOUNDATION AND APPLICATION OF THE MARKET PROFILE eCOURSE

This 11.5 hour eCourse is designed to help you absorb information by seeing it many times, offering the opportunity to play and replay key lessons, observing again and again the context and nuances that can help you trade with less risk.

The first few lessons of this comprehensive eCourse will teach you the basics of understanding the Market Profile, which is as "linear" as we'll get. From there, we'll narrate a variety of real trading days, so you can begin to recognize how the pieces fit together and identify salient Profile configurations: Inside, Rotational, Trend, and Hybrid. We'll also introduce you to "chunking," a proven way to recognize opportunities faster. Chunking is what enables you to back your car out of your garage, walk downstairs, and read a map without having to think about it. In addition to ongoing commentary, there are quizzes to help measure your progress.

As you progress through the eCourse, you'll witness Jim narrating a variety of different trading days in detail as he explains the evolving circumstances of each session. We teach you how to see – what to look for in the market's evolving structure. And more importantly, we help you recognize how the pieces fit together to enable trading with better odds of success.
https://jimdaltontrading.com/product/foundation-course/

ADVANCED NUANCES AND EXCEPTIONS ECOURSE

Advanced Nuances and Exceptions eCourse is for traders who have a solid foundation and understanding of Market Profile and the concepts that Jim teaches, and are looking to fine tune their trading and understand the market nuances, situations and the gotcha moments that are a MUST for any successful trader. This 13-hour eCourse will help you stretch your imagination and guide you in making randomness work for you, aid in helping you understand the market beyond structure, and how context and the interaction of tempo, liquidation, excess, value, and other factors give you clues and an edge in your trading.
https://jimdaltontrading.com/product/advanced-nuances-and-exceptions/

ACKNOWLEDGMENTS

To my son, Rob Dalton: Once again, your gift for communication has elevated our third collaborative endeavor to new heights. Your mastery of language and creativity has allowed me to share my experience with depth, clarity, and emotion. Just as trading is an art, so too is communication. Your nuanced artistic touch has made this book truly special. Thank you for your invaluable contribution.

Beyond helping me express my life's work in this book, Rob has had a successful career as a journalist, writer, and creative director, crafting keynote videos for Microsoft CEO Satya Nadella; helping Starbucks evolve its sustainability story; directing the campaign that made the Boeing 777X the most successful launch in commercial aviation history; writing speeches for executives at Holland America Line, Boeing, NetApp, and Microsoft; building brands for start-ups ranging from climate tech to holographic education; and crafting narratives for organizations like TEDx, the UNDP, and myriad local nonprofits dedicated to improving the world, one story at a time.

Rob can be reached at robertbevandalton@gmail.com.

WindoTrader Corporation and ThinkorSwim (Schwab) for the majority of the charts presented in this book.

CBOT Market Profile, Market Profile is a registered trademark of the Chicago Board of Trade (CBOT), which holds exclusive copyright to the Market Profile graphics. Nothing herein should be considered as a trading recommendation of the Chicago Board of Trade. The views expressed in this publication are exclusively those of Jim Dalton Trading LLC.

ABOUT THE AUTHORS

James Dalton is the founder of Jim Dalton Trading and its predecessor, JDalton Trading. He has more than five decades of experience, including memberships on the Chicago Board of Trade and Chicago Board Options Exchange, where he served as Senior Executive Vice President during its formative years. In the latter part of his markets journey, Jim rejoined UBS Financial Services as Director of Hedge Fund Research – one of the highlights of his career.

Jim's previous two books (*Mind Over Markets* and *Markets in Profile*), written with co-authors Robert B. Dalton and Eric T. Jones, are credited with being peerless in advancing the concepts encompassed by the Market Profile, a powerful tool for organizing time, price, and volume. Over the past three decades, Jim has established himself as an empathetic teacher to individuals and institutions. While many teach trading, Jim's constant refrain is unique: "The most important market you'll trade is yourself – self-understanding is just as important as market understanding."

This book represents the culmination of Jim's teaching and experience. Anyone who has followed him over the years will quickly realize that Jim has continued to advance his teaching methods; he has learned as much from his students as they have learned from him.

The exclamation "*Oorah*" was initially associated with Jim's time in the Marine Corps. Today, "*Oorah*" represents Jim's feelings about this book, his legacy.

Rob Dalton has been a journalist, screenwriter, poet, creative director, and author – each role an embodiment of his ability to build consensus and discover the true heart of the story. Leading by example, Rob engages clients, colleagues, and creative teams in a joyful collaborative exchange that generates powerful ideas to establish meaningful, *actionable* connections. He lives on Bainbridge Island in the great Pacific Northwest with his wife and a dog named George Bailey. His finest creations are his two children (who can already write better than he can).